Classroom Karma

Positive Teaching, Positive Behaviour, Positive Learning

David Wright

David Fulton Publishers

David Fulton Publishers Ltd
The Chiswick Centre, 414 Chiswick High Road, London W4 5TF

www.fultonpublishers.co.uk
www.onestopeducation.co.uk

First published in Great Britain in 2006 by David Fulton Publishers

10 9 8 7 6 5 4 3 2 1

David Fulton Publishers is a division of Granada Learning Limited.

Note: The right of David Wright to be identified as the author of this work has been asserted by him in accordance with the Copyright, Designs and Patents Act 1988.

British Library Cataloguing in Publication Data
A catalogue record for this book is available from the British Library.

ISBN: 1 84312 354 1

References to the gender are used simply to enable the text to flow. Boys and girls are equally capable of behaving in ways described in this book.

All names of students and pupils have been changed.

Typeset by RefineCatch Limited, Bungay, Suffolk
Printed and bound in Great Britain

Contents

This book is dedicated to my family – Maureen, Sean and Jamie – for their thoughts and ideas that have helped me keep this book grounded in the reality of school life. I would also like to express my gratitude to Angela for her ideas and support while I was writing this book.

Also available:

Ways of Learning
Learning Theories and Learning Styles in the Classroom
Alan Pritchard

Get their Attention!
How to Gain Pupils' Respect and Thrive as a Teacher
Sean O'Flynn & Harry Kennedy with Michelle MacGrath

Grammar Survival
A Teacher's Toolkit
Geoff Barton

Introduction

Books and teachers can have many similarities. A book can grab your attention immediately or it can switch you off. A book can open your eyes to the world or send you to sleep. Most of all, certain books have the potential to really lift you, touch your emotions and inspire you to go out and change things in your own life and maybe even the lives of others. That is the aim of this book.

Many say that teaching is an art and that only a small minority have the gift. When we think back to our own time at school, we may have been lucky enough to have had one of those teachers whom we really connected with. They had that special X factor that set them apart from the rest. I believe that there are many more excellent teachers who have not discovered themselves yet. They have still to unlock their potential and touch the lives of the children they teach. This book is one of the keys that could unlock that potential. The ideas and strategies in it will give you the confidence to believe in yourself. When you reach the last page and close the book you will feel different. You will have grown in your understanding and say to yourself, 'Yes, I am ready. I now know what I want to do.'

You cannot tell a good teacher by their appearance – the most unlikely characters can turn out to be marvellous and gifted at capturing the imagination of the children and taking them on a journey that will open their eyes and their minds to the world.

* * *

Before we begin, I would like to tell you a story. I need to take you back to a classroom in 1967. It was full of new children just starting secondary school. They were in the first week of the autumn term. The warm glow of summer was still on the faces of every child and the memories of those long, lazy days out in the open, climbing trees, rolling down grassy verges and picking ripe, juicy blackberries from the hedges were still fresh in our minds.

It was Geography and the teacher was a balding little man, in his early 50s, with a white moustache and glasses. His name was Mr Brown; he was a little odd looking and softly spoken. He did not seem to be like the rest of the teachers who shouted and bellowed down the corridors. What was most incongruous about his image was his shiny blue MGB sports car, but then many middle-aged men get them. Is it something to do with money because when you are young and dashing and could benefit from having a flash car, you can't afford one? Or is it a sign of diminishing virility and a need to reinforce your manhood and potency?

The lesson began with him showing us his map duplicators. These were rubber cylinders that he rolled across a large inkpad and then magically printed out copy after copy of the world map. We all got a map of the world and he set as homework the task of labelling the oceans on it. As he was clearing away the cylinders ready to begin the lesson, he chatted about maps and started to tell us a story.

He was clearing out the attic in his house when he came across a small wooden box tucked away under the eaves in a corner. It must have been left by the previous occupants because the Browns had not seen it when they moved in. Over the years they had put stuff in the attic that they couldn't bear to throw away. A number of years later, they decided to clear out the attic to make a room for Peter, their son, to set up his model railway. Anyway, in the box they discovered a metal tube about six inches long with sealed ends. It was a puzzling object and Mr Brown said he thought it was one of those claves that you use in music. After a few days he realised that there was something inside because he could hear it move as it slid slowly down the tube when it was inverted.

Mr Brown had us captivated as he continued his tale. He told how he tried all sorts of tools to prise off the end and eventually discovered that it was a screw cap that had corroded solid. With the aid of a vice and some mole-grips, he had opened it and tipped out the contents.

There was a pause for effect. We were waiting and guessing. What had he found? He revealed that it was a map made of dirty, brown parchment, with tatty edges. It must have been very old. He showed it to his wife and son, but they did not have any idea where it was. It seemed to be an island and on it was a dotted line leading to a cross. There was no writing and none of the usual signs or symbols you get on maps we have nowadays. They showed it to their neighbours and friends but none of them could identify the island so they gave up.

Some weeks later, Mr Brown had to go up to London so he took the map to a specialist cartographer's in Longacre, Covent Garden. It was a dusty old shop with rolls of maps and atlases everywhere. When he walked in, the doorbell jangled and a funny old man came scurrying out from the stockroom in the back. Mr Brown showed him the map and asked if he knew where the island was.

Suddenly the bell went for the end of the lesson and it was time to pack up and move on to another room. We would have to wait a whole week before we could find out where the island was and what it all meant.

The next lesson came around and Mr Brown could see we were eager to hear more of his story. He pulled down the map of the world and continued his tale. The man in the map shop picked up the map and said, 'It's a tiny little island in the South Pacific.' Mr Brown pointed to it on his map. 'And the reason you couldn't identify it was probably because you were looking at it upside down.' At this point, Mr Brown pulled out the map from his jacket pocket and held it up to show us. 'This is the map,' he announced and we all stretched our necks to get a closer look. 'I had been looking at it like this at first.' Then he turned it round and explained that it did not have a compass on it to indicate north. He pointed to the world map to show us what he meant. He went on to explain the purpose of the compass and the cardinal points. Then he showed us where north was on his map.

The shopkeeper had told him about the tropics and what kind of weather would be found on the island. We were amazed at how much you could get from a map.

Mr Brown discussed the map with his wife and they agreed that he should go on an expedition with his brother to explore the island and find out the significance of the dotted line and the X. They booked their tickets and flew out to Australia. Then they got a seaplane to the bigger island in the group where their hotel was.

The piercing sound of the bell brought us back from the South Sea island paradise to our classroom. The lesson was over already. Mr Brown reminded us about the importance of a compass and told us to add one to our world map for homework.

Geography was only once a week but when it came again the whole class was ready to hear more. Mr Brown checked our homework and explained how the island was on the other side of the equator in the Southern Hemisphere, a long way from the 'civilised world'. He and his brother tried to get a boat out to the island but none of the fishermen was keen. It seemed that the island had some dark secret of the past. The locals were superstitious and told stories of pirates and a native king with his tribe of headhunters. When the pirates came they brought a curse that mysteriously struck down all the natives with a terrible illness. To this day, people rarely go over to the island.

We listened with awe as he described what the fishermen told him. It seemed that their only way over was to hire a boat and sail it themselves. So that is exactly what they did. The next day, Mr Brown and his brother set out. When they beached their little sailing boat and walked up the sand they found they were thwarted by a steep cliff. Mr Brown showed us the contour lines on his map and explained how they represented the hills and valleys. He described their difficult march to where the dotted line began. It was an overgrown path so they had to use machetes to slash their way through the undergrowth. Finally, they reached the spot where they believed the X was.

The bell broke the silence and he did not have time to tell us what they did next. We speculated all week about treasure, skeletons, hidden temples with serpents and the ghost of Blackbeard.

Mr Brown's brother began digging and after a few minutes, hit something hard. Further excavation revealed a small rock chamber with a stone that partially covered its opening. They were so excited they danced around the hole, thinking that it must be treasure and they would be rich beyond their wildest dreams. Mr Brown reached inside the chamber. We all waited in anticipation, no one said a word. We held our breath with excitement.

The chamber turned out to be empty except for a small bag. Whatever else had been in there had been found long ago. All that remained was a tiny bag containing four gold coins. They were so disappointed. In the end they decided to return to their hotel. There was nothing else to do but to fly back to England.

A few weeks after they returned home Mr Brown began to think about the trip again. He may not have found a huge treasure but it had been a great adventure and they did have the coins. He decided to have them made into a pair of cufflinks and then he pulled up his jacket sleeves to show them to us. They glinted in the autumn sun and the large coins had something very old and mysterious about them.

For those four weeks, everyone in the class was swept along with Mr Brown's story. Looking back, we had learned a great deal about maps – the need for a compass, the equator, latitude and longitude, contours and how we can use maps to find out about a place. He continued to use the treasure map for the next few weeks as he taught us about rivers and the effects of erosion on the coastline. We even made a 3D contour map of the island using polystyrene ceiling tiles. It had been a fantastic introduction to secondary school Geography.

Learning is a journey and the teachers lead the children on their pathway to understanding. That story and this book will help you think about that journey. The challenge of creating a positive climate in the classroom is in finding ways of making subjects interesting; capturing the imagination of children; bringing the learning alive and making it real.

This book is divided into three sections. The first two chapters are about how we learn and why most children can behave but some do not. The next section looks at the different styles we can adopt as teachers; what we say and how we say it and the ways of avoiding conflict to ensure all children are included. The final section begins by looking at the values, beliefs and expectations we share as teachers and pupils. It is followed by an examination of the incentives and rewards together with the sanctions and consequences we can use to help children manage their behaviour. The final chapter is about one of the most important aspects of being a teacher. That is, working with our partners.

Teaching can be a lonely experience once you shut the classroom door. Making use of colleague support, the local community and, most of all, the parents can help turn your lessons into really positive, memorable experiences for your pupils. The things that stick in their minds about school are the experiences that are not routine. You owe it to the pupils to unlock your own potential.

David Wright

Chapter 1
How do children learn?

One of the most effective ways of producing a positive atmosphere in the classroom is through the lesson itself. When children are interested in the lesson they will engage with it. Their naturally inquisitive minds will spring to life and they will want to know more. Stimulating, challenging and enjoyable learning experiences will lead to children behaving well and gaining from their time in schools.

Many people believe that we use merely 2% or so of our brain-power – 98% is either wasted or its function is unexplainable. However, the alternative view is that there are specific sites of activity for certain things we do. There are no dead areas and brain scans have revealed activity taking place in different sites depending on the task being carried out. More has been found out about how we learn in the last two decades than ever before, yet the way children are taught and what they are expected to learn has hardly changed. The curriculum and teaching strategies have been dependent on the acquisition of content knowledge using the linguistic learning methods of reading, writing, worksheets, textbooks, copying from the board and assessing with pencil and paper tests. These methods do not take into account any of the new knowledge we have about the brain and how different people prefer to learn.

■ The brain

The central site for learning is called the neo-cortex, which is divided into the left and right hemispheres. These hemispheres work in different ways. Put simply, the left hemisphere processes information in a logical, sequential way, a step at a time while the right hemisphere works holistically, dealing with information in a random way by processing bits that are significant rather than in the order they arrive. The right hemisphere also responds to the more emotive stimuli such as colour, music and pictures. To illustrate this in terms of what is going on in a lesson, the left hemisphere processes the words and sentences of speech while the right hemisphere processes and makes sense of the way it is said. The way you say something, your accent, intonation and expression all contribute to the communication process.

A balanced 'learning diet' should consist of a range of activities and experiences that will stimulate both sides of the brain so that children get the experiences that connect the hemispheres. You could use the following examples when designing lessons:

Left hemisphere	connects to	Right hemisphere
Describe a picture	→	Use diagrams
Learn key words	→	Use a poem, mnemonic or different colours
Change text	→	Into pictures
Produce written descriptions	→	Visualise

The brain is like a muscle and has the same basic requirements including water, fresh air (oxygen) and a good diet (protein). Just like muscles, it needs exercise to make it more powerful. This can be in the form of challenges and stimulating activities. The brain is made up of one million neurons. These are nerve cells that are capable of making connections with each other via dendrites (see Figure 1.1). Learning takes place when a connection is made. The potential is enormous with so many neurons, each capable of making a considerable number of connections in an infinite number of ways.

A neuron sends and receives information. The cells communicate with each other electronically and chemically. The repeated stimulation

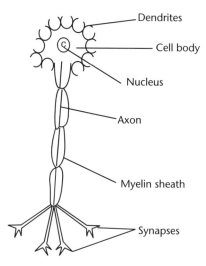

Figure 1.1 Components of a nerve cell

will cause the sender and receiver to get closer so that the connection becomes permanent if they are used frequently. However, pathways will not disappear if they fall into disuse and can be reactivated when required. This is why things we learned when we were younger can come back quite quickly because the pathways are already there.

New things to be learned have to be connected to existing pathways because neurons must connect with other neurons for meaning to be made. Young children will need first-hand experiences in order to connect information because they will not have the connections in place. The brain improves the connections as they are used. This is done by coating the transmitting end with a chemical that renders the connections permanent. Most of this myelination process takes place before the age of sixteen. Smith, A. (1996) believes that:

> *the stages of brain development align roughly with Piaget's observed stages of child development and caution as teachers and educators that we ought not to expect youngsters to function as small adults or with a capability which is biologically out of reach. Learning experiences that are insufficiently developmental and not stimulating bore the youngsters, whereas activities which are beyond their*

capacity given their developmental stage are confusing. The young learner's capacity to handle data and problem solving requires sufficient pathways to be in place. For pathways to be in place requires a plethora of experiences.

The best way to help your pupils make their neuron pathways permanent is to encourage them to take on higher-order thinking skills such as forming opinions about things and then explaining them, interpreting data and then evaluating it rather than just accumulating it, sorting and editing information rather than simply gathering it.

What are the best conditions for learning?

Getting the conditions right so that every child will learn is the challenge, but it can be done. So where do we start? Children will not learn if they are frightened or worried, so your style within the room is important. Stress forms a barrier by causing the body to produce hormones that prepare it to either fight or run. It is a primitive defence mechanism that served human beings well when they were hunter-gatherers. The hormones block the brain's capacity for thought. The sites responsible for personal safety are in readiness. Muscles, lungs and organs are activated to yield a superhuman performance necessary for survival.

The key is to make sure conditions are suitable for learning to take place. Maslow (1999) identified a hierarchy of needs that we require (see Figure 1.2). The basic needs are at the bottom of the pyramid. These include things like warmth, food, drink and clothing. Satisfying these needs is vital. Imagine trying to learn how to write with cold hands, reading out loud when you are really thirsty or concentrating on solving mathematical problems when you are hungry and can only think about when you will get something to eat.

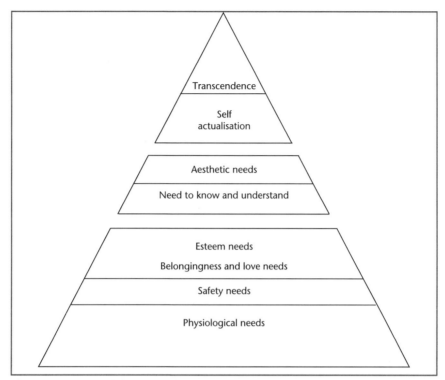

Figure 1.2 Maslow's hierachy of needs (Source: Maslow 1999)

A safe, secure atmosphere in the room will enable you to develop lessons that are high in challenge and low in stress. Children need to believe that it is all right to take risks with their learning. Mistakes should be regarded as opportunities to learn and improve on. A child who does not get it right should be encouraged to try again and not be chastised and criticised.

The work of the memory

Our memories provide a security system to prevent us making the same mistakes again. Memory enables us to access the experiences, knowledge and ideas stored in our brains. We remember things more effectively if they are anchored to familiar experiences or objects. For example, a question on a popular television show was 'Which way round a track do greyhounds run in a race?' I did not know the answer but felt I ought to. I have seen greyhounds race. I visualised the start of the race as the motorised rabbit is released and the gates to the boxes are opened. I ran the 'film clip' in my mind and watched as the greyhounds passed me and veered away to the left as they ran round the first bend. That was it, anti-clockwise!

Children are more likely to remember things if they are contextualised. Not every experience needs to have dramatic, emotional impact but of course when it does the effect can be memorable. That is why visits to historical sites such as a Tudor house or a Victorian classroom with real people in the roles are so popular. Being in the actual building surrounded by the furniture and artefacts helps bring the experience to life.

You do not have to leave the classroom to make learning effective. There are many ways that it can be done through role-plays, practical tasks and experiments. Experiences that require the use of two or more senses will open up pathways in the brain and cause connections between neurons to become more permanent.

What's in it for me?

This is the question that we probably all ask at one time or another. Why do something, especially if it is not enjoyable? There has got to be a point. Children can quickly become turned off if there does not seem to be a reason for learning something. Once this happens they will probably not be able to remember what the teacher was trying to teach them. Motivation improves the memory and increases the efficiency of learning. When we want something enough we will do whatever is needed to get it. So how does this happen in the classroom?

It is all in the desire to want to get better. Practising something often enough will eventually result in an improvement. The repetitive nature of practice strengthens the connections and leads to a more automatic response. The playing of a musical instrument is a good example of this. If you keep practising a piece then you will eventually be able to play it without needing to look at the sheet music.

The challenge for teachers is how to motivate children. Pre-school-aged children come out with many questions such as:

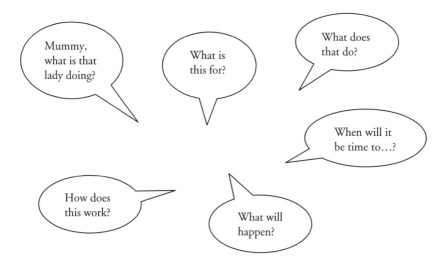

Teachers place a lot of emphasis on getting answers from children to check whether they have remembered what has been taught. The difficulty with this approach is that it dulls their inquisitive urge. What we need to do is reverse this and provide for more opportunities for children to investigate, inquire and talk about new things. Help them ask questions rather than give the answers.

The class is studying the discovery of the New World. What sorts of questions might they ask the sailors returning from the Americas? This kind of approach gets the children thinking about the topic or idea and working out what they want to find out.

Questions are often far more important than answers. The world is changing rapidly and children need to be equipped with skills that will help them deal with a very different way of living. Our knowledge is rapidly becoming redundant and much of what we learned is now useless, such as imperial measurements and log tables. In a few years' time video recorders will probably have disappeared and maybe even computer mice. Faced with such dramatic changes, children will need new skills, not loads of facts. They will need to be able to solve problems that do not even exist yet. To do this they will have to return to the basic starting point of asking questions like:

What is it?
What does it do?
Why is it like this?
What happens if I do this?
When will it happen?
How does it work?

Why are we learning this?

There has to be a reason for doing something and learning new things in school is no different. Secondary-aged children can often be persuaded that it is to help them pass their examinations or as a means to an end. If they get good grades they could become a doctor, vet, etc. The objective is to help children find a reason that will motivate them to engage with the lesson, the 'what's in it for me?' factor. This can be done in a number of ways and primary pupils do not necessarily need extrinsic rewards like good grades or career promises. It is more about helping them to become interested in the world they live in and putting the curriculum content into a context for them. The trick is to make the subject appealing through the structure and delivery.

New topics are best begun with an explanation of the big picture to help the pupils think about what they will get from studying it. Making the learning goal clear is vital. It enables the pupils to set themselves a target and with practice and encouragement they will eventually be able to do the same for all subjects.

Help the children to think about their own learning goals. Show them how they set targets when they do things in their own leisure time like trying to reach a new level in a PlayStation game. Encourage them to take a few minutes to set a target for learning in the lesson or an activity, e.g. PE may be about invasion games and you are teaching hockey. Help them to consider what they can and want to do such as dribble the ball or pass accurately. This part of the lesson is vital but an evaluation also needs to take place at the end. 'Did I achieve my goal? If not, what do I need to do to get there?'

A child who is motivated will pursue a clear route from their desire to do something through to the acquisition of knowledge or the skill they seek. They will push themselves to overcome any barriers they encounter because they want to succeed. Children who do not see the point of doing something and have no desire to do it will make comments like 'It's boring!' We cannot force children to learn but we can improve the conditions for learning so they are more likely to be motivated.

A common view among disaffected children is that education is being done to them. They feel they have little choice or involvement in the learning and in many cases they may not even be able to access it because they have below-average levels of ability and the activities have not been differentiated enough to enable them to achieve and be successful. It is hardly surprising that a child who has learning delay, is possibly dyspraxic and has a reading age two or more years lower than the rest of the class will find the work inaccessible and give up if the teacher's efforts to include them are not working. The result is likely to be a switched-off child who will cause problems.

Give them hope

The solution is to make the task appear possible for all levels of ability. The main barrier to motivation is a sense of hopelessness – 'Why should I bother if I am going to fail?' Give them hope because success is dependent on:

- emotional feelings of belief – 'If I try it I will be able to do it and feel good at the end';

- a sense of security – 'If I have a go and get it wrong I will not get criticised or chastised.'

This is achieved by helping the child to see a new learning experience as a challenge that they cannot do yet but will be able to do in time. They may have to make mistakes but that is okay because they will be able to learn from them. Mistakes are a good thing, not something to feel bad about.

Being successful

Children will be motivated once they have experienced the rewards of being successful. Success can become addictive if the child enjoys the praise and recognition they get from you and their peers. Equally, getting it wrong may lead to negative feelings of failure and resignation. That is why it is important to keep the level of challenge in perspective.

No hope	⟶	resignation
Hope	⟶	learn from mistakes and try again
Too much challenge	⟶	little or no learning
Appropriate challenge	⟶	an urge to have a go because there is a good chance of success

Involving the pupils

Children will be motivated if they feel they are being involved. Teachers who try to teach at the children by talking, lecturing, dictating and getting them to copy off the board will end up with a class being passive and unable to engage with the learning. Children will gain far more from the lesson when they are given choices and are allowed to contribute their opinions and evaluate their achievements. Teachers who value these qualities will be able to enhance the learning process for their class.

Being ready to learn

Motivating the pupils is not the only barrier teachers face. The children will have their own internal ones. They may have emotional barriers such as feelings of anger and frustration, loss, grievance, depression and distraction brought about by events at home. They may have physical difficulties that prevent them concentrating. These include hunger, thirst or illness. There may be clinical barriers such as Attention Deficit Hyperactivity Disorder (ADHD), Obsessive Compulsive Disorder (OCD) or autism. External barriers could include discomfort caused by conditions in the room, inappropriate teaching methods or relationship problems.

Any of these could manifest as a lack of motivation or poor or inappropriate behaviour. Some of them can be addressed with very little extra effort or resources; others will require the help of professionals. Let's look at the ones that can be addressed within the classroom.

Getting the teaching methods right for the children

Howard Gardner (1993) proposed that we all learn in different ways and we have preferred learning styles that can be broadly described as:

- visual – who prefer to learn by seeing;

- auditory – who prefer to learn by hearing and using sounds;

- kinaesthetic – who prefer to learn by doing.

29% of us are predominantly visual learners, 34% are auditory learners and 37% are kinaesthetic learners (Garnett, S. 2002). We are, of course, able to learn by other methods as well. Therefore, it is important to provide children with activities that utilise all three styles so they will learn and develop new skills

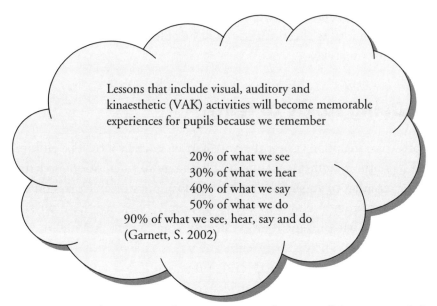

Lessons that include visual, auditory and kinaesthetic (VAK) activities will become memorable experiences for pupils because we remember

20% of what we see
30% of what we hear
40% of what we say
50% of what we do
90% of what we see, hear, say and do
(Garnett, S. 2002)

Once you have got to know your pupils you will be aware of the kinds of activities they prefer and excel at.

Visual learners

They learn most effectively by seeing things. They like:

Drawing	News reports
Writing	Television
Posters	Films, videos, DVDs
Interactive whiteboards	Interactive displays
Wall displays	Overhead transparencies
Graphs	Computers
Diagrams	Pictures
Books	Mind maps
Diaries	Flow charts
Letters	Arrow charts
Keywords	Maps and atlases

They also tend to gesticulate and speak with their hands. When they do talk it is quietly.

Auditory learners

They learn most effectively through sound and hearing activities like:

Circle time	Dance
Hot seating	Drama
Show and tell	Reporting
Audio tapes	Debates
Radio programmes	Discussion
Music and sound effects	Interviews
Stories read to them	

They give and receive instructions verbally. They like to listen to music and may sing or hum while doing things.

Kinaesthetic learners

They learn most effectively through movement. They like:

Role-playing and dressing up

Hot seating	Flap and pop-up books
Envoying	Music and movement
Jigsawing	Cut up and re-arranging
Show and tell	Murals
Making things	Game stations
Modelling and collage	Outdoor pursuits
Gym	PE
Performances	Dance
	Brain gym

How do I find out a child's preferred learning style?

There are numerous assessment tools available for doing this and one easy-to-use method is given on the following page. However, there is no substitute for your own conclusions based on careful observations. To come to an accurate, informed decision requires both the personal opinions and observations of staff who work with the children and the more empirical findings obtained using a questionnaire (see Photocopiable materials). Questionnaires can either be given to the children to complete on their own, can be done with a parent or completed by two members of staff working together.

Each answer reveals a specific preference. For example, if the answer to the first question is 'Yes' then that points towards an auditory learning style. When you evaluate a child's scores you may find they have similar or the same scores for two of the categories, e.g. Auditory = 7, Visual = 7. This points to the child being comfortable learning with either style.

Kinaesthetic learners will say 'yes' to question numbers:

| 3 | 5 | 6 | 7 | 12 | 17 |

Visual learners will say 'yes' to:

| 2 | 4 | 9 | 13 | 14 | 15 | 18 |

Auditory learners will say 'yes' to:

| 1 | 8 | 10 | 11 | 16 | 19 | 20 |

N.B you do not count 'no' responses

(After Garnett, S. 2002)

It is better not to tell the children what their preferred learning style is because they could typecast themselves and not want to expand their skills. Once you have the information about your pupils you will need to plan lessons with activities that suit their specific learning styles but also help them develop the other ones. For example, using kinaesthetic activities such as making things could help auditory learners. Let's look at an example of how this can be achieved in a lesson.

■ Finding out a child's preferred learning style

Name.. Class......... Date............

1. I like listening to music   Yes   No
2. I like drawing   Yes   No
3. I like moving about   Yes   No
4. I like watching films   Yes   No
5. I like dancing   Yes   No
6. I like acting   Yes   No
7. I like making things   Yes   No
8. I like chatting to people   Yes   No
9. I like reading   Yes   No
10. I like discussing things   Yes   No
11. I like showing and telling the class about things   Yes   No
12. I like going on trips   Yes   No
13. I like making posters   Yes   No
14. I like writing   Yes   No
15. I like drawing diagrams   Yes   No
16. I like talking while I work   Yes   No
17. I like to go outside for lessons   Yes   No
18. I like to watch videos in lessons   Yes   No
19. I like listening to stories   Yes   No
20. I like to speak to my friends   Yes   No

(After Garnett, S. 2002)

Little Red Riding Hood

This lesson is about a re-telling of the traditional fairy story. You will need to arrange your class into groups with four pupils in each.

Group roles: Narrator, Wolf, Little Red Riding Hood, Granny.

Visual activity

The pupils read the story and identify the locations where each scene takes place, e.g.:

the woods

cottage living room

cottage bedroom.

Design the stage sets for a puppet play. Each set should include the backdrop and any props such as trees, bushes or furniture. Do a plan view to show where each item is positioned and a sketch of what the audience will see. Then make the sets. This could be extended as an art project.

Auditory activity

Re-write the story as a script for the narrator and characters. Include directions for each character and any notes about the stage such as 'dim lights'. The characters then practise the play. If you have tape recorders you could record their readings and listen to them to help them improve.

Kinaesthetic activity

Each group makes finger or sock puppets for the characters in their play and then practises using them by rehearsing the play.

VAK activities

The narrator and the cast perform the story to the rest of the class or to a video camera.

How do I help children remember more?

We remember more from the beginnings and endings of things than what happens in the middle (Hughes, M. 1999). This is called the *primacy and recency effect* and can be used to improve what children retain from lessons. When children enter a classroom they will be expecting something to happen. This is the ideal time to deliver the main learning point because their attention and concentration will be heightened. Figure 1.3 shows how the chance of learning something begins to fall off as time passes but can rise again as the lesson comes to an end. If you can make the starts of your lessons special the children will become accustomed to expecting something and be alert and ready.

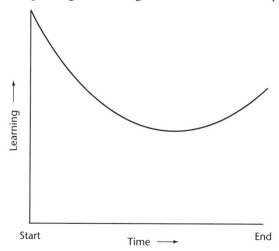

Figure 1.3 The primacy and recency effect

Think about your own lesson beginnings and what you do. Do you call the register, get the children to fold their arms and wait in silence, hand back homework, distribute books, have an oral starter that is unrelated to the lesson topic, give the big picture and then discuss the work done and where it goes next? If you do two or more of these you will probably not be getting to the main learning point until fifteen minutes into the lesson and the advantage of heightened anticipation, attention and concentration will be lost.

So how can a teacher make use of this?

The children are ready and their attention is on you so capture the moment. Tell them what you want them to remember or do something that shows them what you want them to know in the first few minutes of the lesson. This does not mean you have to explain it and go in to detail. Get the key fact, learning point or idea into their minds as soon as you have their attention by *headlining* (see Figure 1.4).

Any number multiplied by 10 will
always end in a zero

$$5 \times 10 = 5\underline{0}$$

$$7 - 10 = 7\underline{0}$$

All sentences start with a capital
letter and end in a full stop

$$\underline{T}he \ cat \ drank \ the \ milk\underline{.}$$

The Battle of Hastings took place in

1066

Figure 1.4 Examples of headlining

Deliver the main learning point before you do anything else, even before you say 'hello', and use VAK methods. Appeal to their senses.

The explanations will come later. What you are doing is very similar to what a journalist does. You are giving the headline which grabs the pupils' attention in the same way a newspaper story does, e.g.:

VOLCANO ERUPTS

Then give the story and explain who, what, where, when and why later.

Headline the main learning points within the first three minutes.

Endings of both lessons and activities are times when interest levels rise, so recalling what has been studied in that time will pay off. Recall should be brief and concise so confine it to reviewing the key points. Break down the review into keywords to engage both sides of the brain.

Figure 1.5 shows how recall near the end of a lesson can fix something in the memory but it soon fades with time until very little of what was taught can be remembered.

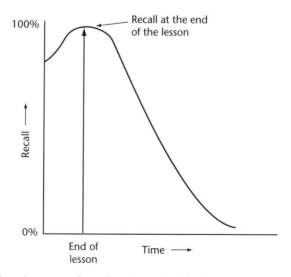

Figure 1.5 The advantage of recall at the end of the lesson

- ■ Write the review points on the board in different colours.
- ■ Place them in a memorable picture or a diagram.
- ■ Create a rhyme or acronym for them.
- ■ Children tell each other the main point.

If you repeat the review in the same way at the end of the day as home-work, then a day later and then the following week, it will fix it more effectively in the memory. Figure 1.6 illustrates this. Note that there is a gradual decline with each recall but the overall result is higher reten-tion than if none had taken place.

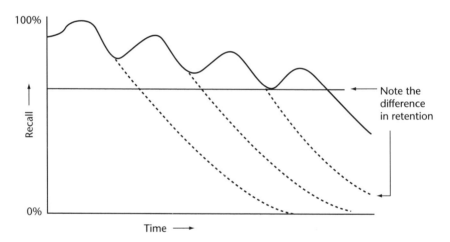

Figure 1.6 How recall can make a difference to retention

Bite-size bits

How do you eat an elephant?
A bit at a time.

An hour-long lesson can really drag for some children if the activity doesn't vary. As a rule, a child can usually concentrate on something for their age + 2 minutes, so a 6 year old will be able to concentrate for 8 minutes and an 11 year old should be able to concentrate for 13 minutes. If you plan your tasks with this in mind you will have between two and four tasks during the individual/group work section of the lesson.

Each task is a new beginning which allows you to capitalise on the renewed attention the pupils will give. There will also be a chance to briefly review at the end of the tasks so you will be able to build more reviews into the whole lesson. This will result in even more opportunities to consolidate and commit to longer-term memory what has been learned.

Take breaks between tasks

The children will make more of the lesson if they are able to take mini-breaks between tasks. These need only be 1–2 minutes long. The break allows the pupils to disconnect from the subject. A good way of doing this is to utilise the brain gym activities that are available. Activities that require physical and mental concentration will help motor coordination and engage the whole brain.

> *Research into Kinesiology suggests that regular use of brain gym activities can alleviate stress, improve hand-eye coordination, concentration on focused activities and quicken the response to visual stimuli.*
>
> *(Smith, A. 1996:70)*

Activities should require different movements for the left and the right hands and fingers. They could be:

- drawing something in the air while saying out loud something else;
- learning sign language;
- relaxation and breathing exercises;
- physical flexing exercises.

Brain gym exercises provide ideal breaks and allow new activities to take place with an increased level of expectation.

The brain seems to have specific sites of activity for certain things we do.

The left side of the brain processes logical sequences.

The right side of the brain works in a holistic way.

Lessons should include activities that stimulate both sides of the brain.

People have preferred learning styles: visual, auditory and kinaesthetic.

REVIEW

Break the learning into bite-size chunks.

Introduce key learning points within the first 3 minutes of the lesson.

Recalling what has been taught reinforces learning. Aim to recall key points in later lessons.

We remember more at the beginning and end, so create lots of new beginnings in lessons.

Give pupils 'brain breaks' to improve concentration and coordination.

AND FINALLY... An essential factor in reducing poor behaviour and producing a good learning environment is with lessons that are challenging and enjoyable.

Chapter 2

Why do some children behave and some do not?

▨ Introduction

Close your eyes and imagine the perfect class. Every child is working on activities they are clearly enjoying. There is a buzz in the atmosphere. It is one of enthusiasm and industry. Children share ideas, discuss their learning and know what they are trying to achieve. They have talked about the work together as a class and the teacher has helped them identify the criteria for the tasks. They will know they have achieved the desired outcome and the teacher will evaluate it to look for improvements. Every child is satisfied with their own progress because they do not view learning as a competition with their peers. To them it is a personal journey that will open up the world. One of the most prized aspects of this utopian class is the ability to ask questions. It is useful to imagine how you want things to be. Then it is simply a matter of working out how to achieve it.

The reality for many teachers is that there will be a mixed bag of children. Most will be good but there will be a number who could be challenging. The teacher will have to solve countless little problems, difficulties and disagreements. They will have to answer lots of questions about the work: what happened the day before, what's happening tomorrow, what's happening in the world and why is so-and-so doing this or that? With so much going on and so many demands it is not surprising that it does not always go right even for the most experienced.

Children do not set out to be naughty. Most are intrinsically good and want to please, but they all have the potential to stray. We need to try to understand what prompts some children to misbehave so that we can respond in ways that will avoid conflicts and help them to improve. There is no mystery about how this can be achieved, it is simply a case of planning what you will do in different circumstances and adopting strategies that prevent spontaneous and irrational responses that inevitably result in emotionally charged, negative reactions.

In this chapter we will look at why children misbehave from three perspectives:

■ the position of the pupil;

■ the family context;

■ the school's influence.

We will then consider the notion of special needs and how requirements for individual children can best be met.

■ The pupils

An individual child may have specific clinical reasons that affect their behaviour. These include:

■ blindness or partial sight;

■ deafness or difficulty hearing;

■ speech difficulties;

■ mobility difficulties.

In the past, children with these difficulties were described as 'handicapped' or disabled and would usually have been educated in special schools. With the advent of a more open, inclusive attitude they are much more likely to receive their education in mainstream schools. Governments have required schools to make provision for these pupils. Consequently, changes have been made to the physical structures of the buildings to ensure the children have access. There are also many technical aids available including personal microphones connected to hearing aids, concept keyboards and speech-creating computers. Teachers and support staff can be trained in the use of sign language and Braille versions of a wide range of books can be obtained.

There are other clinical conditions that affect behaviour and educationalists are becoming far more aware of them.

Attention disorders

There are a number of these. Perhaps the most well known is Attention Deficit Hyperactivity Disorder and it can become a huge barrier to learning for a child and also the others in the class. The main feature is the child's inability to concentrate on an activity for an extended period of time. It is most common in boys and can be transmitted genetically. A third of all fathers who had ADHD have children with it. Once diagnosed, a child may be placed on medication, which is designed to help them concentrate in school. However, the problem is not often diagnosed until the child is well into their primary education. The signs to look for include many but not all of the following:

- difficulty in concentrating or focusing on-tasks and being easily distracted;

- low self-esteem because peers get fed up with his behaviour;

- overactive, fidgets or squirms;

- difficulty taking turns;

- blurting out answers to questions;

- difficulty following instructions;

- noisy when playing;

- talking excessively;

- often interrupts;

- loses things;

- engages in dangerous behaviour.

Strategies for dealing with children with ADHD

- Make sure tasks are short. The ideal length is the age of the child plus two minutes for a normal child, e.g. eight years = ten minutes. For a child with ADHD this should be shorter. Limit most tasks to around five minutes.
- Reward the child for staying on-task and completing it.
- Explain the task carefully and make sure the child understands what to do. It may be useful to break up a five-minute task into three steps and give the instructions separately, e.g. Step 1 give instructions – then complete the work, Step 2 give instructions then complete the work.
- ADHD children are often kinaesthetic learners so give them appropriate activities to help them channel their energy constructively.
- Pair the child up with another responsible pupil and ask them to help in keeping the child on-task.
- Watch out for the signs and intervene when you see the child going off-task.
- Provide time-management support. Help the child to watch a clock so they will get an idea of how long common activities usually last.
- Avoid copying-out activities as ADHD children do not write quickly or accurately.
- Help the child keep the table tidy and organised.
- Set up a personal checklist for the day.
- Build movement into the lesson. For example, the child could come and show you how much they have done every ten minutes.
- Find alternative consequences to detention at break to enable the child to get physical exercise and a change of scenery.

Hyperactivity

This is a medical condition that may possibly be aggravated by things like food, drink and additives. Much has already been written about potential links with certain foods with chemical additives and the changes they apparently bring about in behaviour. You may have drawn your own conclusions from observing children after they have had particular foods for lunch.

The strategies used to help a child with ADHD will be effective for children with a tendency to be hyperactive. It is also worth mentioning the food and drink that your class consume at breaks and lunchtimes. Work can be done in Science and PSHE as part of the Healthy Schools Programme on the benefits of a balanced diet and exercise. Classes and school councils can take a role in developing whole-school exercise programmes and menus for dinners. They can also be involved in discussions around the contents of a healthy packed lunch, tuck shops and the availability of fresh water and milk.

Autism and Asperger's Syndrome

Children with autism can exhibit behaviour that ranges from being barely noticeable to the extreme where they seem distant and unreachable. When it is that severe they are described as being in a world of their own. The milder form of autism, known as Asperger's Syndrome, is the more common in mainstream schools. A child with this condition may exhibit any number of the following characteristics:

■ fixed in their ways and very dogmatic;

■ gaze avoidance – does not make eye contact;

■ socially inept;

■ unaware of the way conversation is developing, resulting in unrelated comments and interruptions;

■ physically weak with poor coordination;

■ unexplainable outbursts of anger;

■ unable to deal with changes in routines;

- fussy eater;

- has to wear specific items of clothing and certain colours;

- cannot tolerate certain sounds, loud noise, colours, smells;

- reading may be advanced but abstract comprehension is absent;

- evidence of creativity in sophisticated work but this may actually be extremely accurate replication of things remembered, e.g. well-drawn, detailed pictures of buildings;

- photographic memory;

- phenomenal ability to calculate, e.g. can compute quickly or provide days and dates for exact years.

Autism can vary and is described as a spectrum. Children cannot be easily diagnosed and so caution should be taken not to assume that they are autistic simply because they present with some of these behaviours.

Strategies for dealing with children with Asperger's Syndrome

Children who have either been diagnosed with Asperger's Syndrome or are showing some of the behaviours described earlier can be helped using a range of strategies. It is unlikely that you will be able to change their behaviour or responses but you will be able to help them be more included in what the whole class do if you adapt around their needs. There is a wide variety of strategies so only a selection is listed here.

- Provide a timetable of the day's events including activities not shown on the curriculum timetable.

- Alert the child as soon as possible of any potential staff changes or activities.

- Signal the end of activities, tasks, lessons, etc. five minutes before they actually end so the child knows they must finish what they are doing.

- Do not challenge the child in the same way as you would when other children misbehave. Do not insist they look at you when you are talking to them. If they are doing something different to what you asked or expected, talk to them about it. Autistic children will interpret instructions literally. Their actions may appear to be deliberate acts of mischief or cheekiness but in fact they are alternative ways of doing things. For example, if the teacher asks the class to write something under the title, an autistic child may turn to the next page and write it on the top line so it is literally under the title (on the other side of the sheet).

- Do not pressure the child to take all the food at lunch. They may feel they can eat only certain things or be unable to tolerate having certain foods like baked beans touching the fish. The child will not starve or go hungry so it is better not to get into a conflict over it.

- Work may be untidy or some activities done in an unsatisfactory way such as PE or swimming. The child may lack the coordination to do them any better so see their efforts for what they are.

- Provide a safe haven for the child during playtimes. Allow them to come off the playground if things get difficult. Children with Asperger's are possible targets for bullying.

- Social stories can be used to help them work through various problems that we would solve by being aware of the signs and feelings of others.

Tourette's Syndrome

This is a relatively rare disorder of movement named after the French neurologist Gilles de la Tourette who first described it in 1885. It begins in childhood with repetitive tics and facial grimaces. Involuntary grunts and other noises may start as the disease takes hold. In around 50% of cases, the sufferer has episodes of foul language.

It is more common in males and often undiagnosed because of its strange symptoms. It is a life-long condition but can be helped with medication. Many children at primary school may exhibit nervous tics and movement difficulties that are not Tourette's Syndrome. However, a child presenting with many of these symptoms may be in the early stages of the disease.

Non-clinical reasons for poor behaviour

There are many reasons why a child may not behave appropriately. Serious misbehaviour is a cry for help. The child is anxious and stressed and is not able to talk about their worries so they seek attention in other ways.

Poor self-esteem

This can be associated with many of the clinical conditions described earlier but it is also a common factor in many of the children who have difficulties with their behaviour at school. There are some children who have a personality trait that prevents them from coping with the attention they encounter. They are shy and do not like being put on the spot and in the public eye. When a teacher asks them a question or praises them in front of the whole class they go into meltdown because they are so embarrassed. They will not misbehave in a defiant way but their response may seem like non-compliance.

Then there are the children who do not get a return on their studies and see themselves as 'thick'. They are no good at sport and do not excel at any other hobbies or activities. They try to gain respect in order to boost their self-image by being a class clown or a bully. They are victims of a system that compares one pupil with another. Rendall and Stuart (2005) argue that there are a number of domains to self-esteem. A child may have a good self-image in some domains of their life such as among peers, with their family or of relationships or activities like sport. It is in the school-based domains of academic work that low self-esteem and poor self-image are most likely to occur.

The 'boundary tester'

Some children develop an urge to test the teacher to find out how far they can push the boundaries. There may be a legitimate reason for doing this. It could be that the child is very insecure and needs to know that the teacher has strong boundaries that will provide security. There are children who want the opposite: they want to know how much freedom they are allowed. They will go to the wire and beyond to see what happens. A firm response will probably end further testing, as they will learn where the boundary is.

Poor motivation

You cannot please all the people all of the time. There will be occasions when a child is bored. You may try everything you can think of to make the work fun and engaging but the task, the subject or school itself does not seem to interest the child on a particular day. The result will be that they disengage and look for their own ways to alleviate their boredom. This is when the trouble occurs.

Peer pressure

Young children in a school setting suddenly find themselves outside the safety and security of the family home. They are independent from their parents and face a new, daunting challenge of the classroom with its rules and competition for attention of other pupils. The sense of being alone and unsure of things motivates many children to align themselves with the peer group. They are looking for normality and a feeling of belonging that they get when they become part of a group.

Hierarchies develop in classrooms and children become subjected to the pressure of the peer group. It can be a positive force but it also has its negative side when individual members of the group get coerced into doing foolish things. This can lead to bullying and abuse if it goes unchecked. Peer pressure can be powerful and can transcend the authority of the teacher, the school and even the parents.

Rifts and rivalries

Children can be the best of friends one minute and then total enemies the next. Arguments and conflicts can occur for what would seem to be the most trivial of reasons. Disagreements develop because of possessions, games or who is in or out of a friendship group. Feuds break out and cause rifts that can lead to quite serious fights that you will have to deal with. Knowing what is going on in the class is important if you are to maintain order and keep the peace.

A potential area of conflict is the arrival of a new pupil. They may challenge the existing hierarchy and upset the equilibrium. One way of preventing this is to have a class order and any newcomer is placed at the end, at least for the first term. This reduces the likelihood of any jostling for power because stability is achieved when everyone knows and accepts their place.

No self-control

A lot of silly behaviour in young children is due to their lack of self-control and not deliberate defiance, as some teachers would believe. They have not fully developed their social awareness and when they find themselves in certain situations they do not know how to behave properly. Changes in routine, meeting new people, moving rooms or getting brand new equipment can trigger excitable behaviour. It may be a way of concealing the nervousness they feel. The significant message of this book is to acquire the strategies to help children develop their self-control.

The 'out there' culture

It is very common for children involved in incidents to see themselves as victims. They look to blame others for things that they were involved in. They do not accept responsibility for their own behaviour. The key strategy promoted in this book is to get children to take that responsibility. This is achieved by helping them understand how their actions can have an impact on the outcome and making them aware of their choices. There are many new resources available in schools including the National Primary Strategy 'Social and Emotional Aspects of Learning' pack (2005). The purpose behind the activities in the pack is to help children consider questions like 'What did I do?', 'What choices do I have?', 'How do I feel about . . . ?' and 'How will it affect others?' The resources can be used in assemblies, circle time, PSHE and curriculum lessons.

▨ The family

The family dynamics and the home can be a major factor in determining a child's behaviour. The level of stability and the parents' attitudes towards their children must have an influence.

The critical incident

Children who do not have a clinical reason for their behavioural difficulties must have another cause that triggers them. Significant numbers of troubled children appear to have experienced some kind of critical incident. The sorts of trauma likely to be at the root of their problems might include:

■ parents divorcing;

■ witnessing parents arguing or fighting;

■ parent addiction to alcohol or drugs;

■ parental depression;

■ disowned or neglected by a parent;

■ redundancy or long-term unemployment of a parent;

■ witnessing abuse or being abused;

■ family member going through a serious illness;

■ bullied at home or in school;

■ involvement in crime or drugs;

■ family member convicted of a crime or in prison;

■ refugee from a war zone.

The *Framework for the Assessment of Children in Need and their Families* (Department of Health 2000) provides a useful starting point for considering the triggers for challenging behaviour (see Figure 2.1).

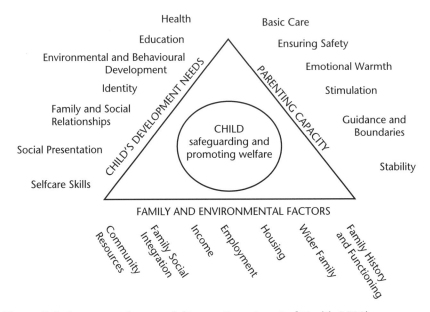

Figure 2.1 Assessment framework (Source: Department of Health 2000)

Exactly how such traumatic events lead to poor behaviour is not the subject of this book, but it would seem that there is more than a coincidental link.

Poor levels of care

The mental and physical well-being of the young dependant is the responsibility of the parent/carer. Inadequate levels of care lead to problems in the physical and cognitive development of the child and their behaviour. It is not uncommon for some children to come to school without having had any breakfast. They may be dishevelled, dirty and even have nits. Their home life is probably quite chaotic and there may be many reasons why their parents do not care for them adequately. However, that does not stop these children from feeling hungry or being uncomfortable in their dirty clothes. They may not be able to explain why they are unsettled but their behaviour usually reflects their feelings.

Parents who send their children to school with poorly prepared packed lunches will be inadvertently contributing to classroom problems. Processed foods are convenient and easily obtainable but may well be of low nutritional value. They contain high levels of additives which some believe contributes to hyperactivity in young children. Then there are children with very little in their lunch boxes. They have barely enough calories to see them through the day and what they do have is of poor quality. Staff who discover children with inadequate amounts of food usually manage to conjure up something extra to help, but longer-term solutions are required. The opposite to this are the over-fed children who eat far too much and do insufficient exercise. They spend long periods of time sitting down watching television or playing computer games. In the end their weight becomes a barrier and they find they cannot do active things. Children who get into this situation become targets for bullying because they are different from the rest.

Abuse and neglect

In tragic cases, poor care develops into serious neglect. This may occur when the parent/carer has suffered a critical incident such as the death of a loved one, a serious illness or a separation, any of which may be accompanied by depression and an over-use of drugs or alcohol. The signs become noticeable in the child. At its worst they lack energy, are unwashed and exhibit sudden changes in behaviour. There may be marks on their bodies and unexplained absences.

Children taken into care after being badly abused will not immediately change and behave normally again. Sometimes their experiences are so traumatic that they cause serious psychological effects and they need professional help.

Very aggressive and challenging children are likely to be frightened and anxious. They may have lost control of many aspects of their life and feel helpless. They search around for things they can control such as school and their peers, which eventually leads to aggressive acts.

▨ **The school and the teachers**

We can have little impact on what happens at home. However, children are at school for six hours a day, five days a week, for thirty-nine weeks of the year. This is a significant amount of time to modify any inappropriate behaviour.

The question that needs consideration is whether school, as an experience for young people, is also a cause of poor behaviour. There are many incidents in school but they do not all involve children with troubled backgrounds. Children are often required to sit for long periods in crowded, uncomfortable conditions, performing written tasks and furnishing the answers to countless questions. Given the numbers of children involved, it is not surprising that they misbehave. Obviously, children with clinical conditions or complicated home lives have the potential to contribute to the problems, but the role of the teacher cannot be ruled out.

When the Labour Government took office in 1997 it placed education at the heart of its reforms. A great deal of emphasis was put on raising achievement and this produced significant tensions between schools, local authorities and the Government itself. Measurable outcomes were prioritised in the form of results and targets in the push to improve standards in state schools. Parsons (1999) describes a continuum that schools can be positioned on that ranges from a social, democratic and humanist approach through to a controlling one. Schools that prioritise values such as high academic standards, a traditional curriculum and a controlled school population tend to be less tolerant of difference and expect conformity. Rendall and Stuart (2005) argue that such schools give

> *a lower priority to the pastoral role including the opportunity to address individual children's strengths in areas other than the traditional subjects.*

The unspoken expectation is that a teacher should be able to control their class. However, the degree of preparation that teachers get for this can vary, which leads to the development of many different approaches.

The variations in styles of behaviour management, coupled with variations in ethos, give rise to significant ambiguity and even confusion among staff and children about what is required. Caulby and Harper (1985) argue that the way a school is organised can affect pupil behaviour. In particular, they link it to the school ethos. The way the staff approach the management of behaviour can determine the level of misbehaviour and can even be a significant cause of it. The following pages briefly describe some of the factors concerning us as teachers that can affect the way children behave in our classes.

Inconsistency and unfairness

Many children develop very strong moral values including a good sense of what is right and wrong. They are able to spot inconsistencies and expect them to be addressed. When an inconsistency occurs children perceive it as an injustice. A good example of this is when a class are told to line up quietly and a child messes around. The teacher spots it but does not give the child a consequence. A few minutes later another child does the same thing and the teacher loses her patience. She gets more cross with the second child, tells them she is fed up with being ignored and gives them a detention. This inconsistent approach is clearly unfair.

The self-fulfilling prophecy

We make judgements about people within seconds of meeting them. First impressions are based upon a complex set of assessments of the visual signs we receive. As teachers, we may be told about a particular child or class prior to taking them. This information can be useful because it allows us to consider how we can best serve the children we teach. It may also have a detrimental effect. We may be told that a child has been poorly behaved, which prejudices our view before we have even met them.

Children will respond to us and the ways we treat them. Talking up a class or an individual child will make them feel good and start to believe in themselves. Conversely, using negative comments and phrases like 'You are always the one who starts it . . .' or 'I might have known it would be you who was to blame' will be demotivating and the child may eventually just give up. They will feel they can never do anything right in your eyes and become what you are labelling them. It is important to keep an open mind and approach every child positively by building in strategies to help them change rather than write them off.

Being confrontational

One style that some teachers adopt is to be oppressive. They believe that they are in charge and the children should not challenge their authority. When a child does, they are dealt with in a confrontational and often aggressive way. The effect on the child is to either frighten them into submission or provoke them into defiance. Either way brings no real advantages, only difficulties (see Chapter 1: How do children learn?). Confrontation is not a solution and is a barrier in the development of a positive, calm climate that is conducive to learning.

Weak responses

The opposite to the aggressive style is the passive response. The teacher will try to persuade pupils to follow directions and they will detect a weakness of character and exploit it. The passive teacher will fail to show they are the leader in the classroom and the result will be unruly children doing their own thing. Weak responses to incidents leave an uncertain void. Children expect adults to take control to resolve problems. They do not expect a lack of response.

Sour or bad-tempered moments

Everybody has their off-days and teachers are no exception. We need to guard against our emotions taking control during these times. That is why a well-thought-through behaviour plan is essential. It will enable you to use procedures to manage difficult situations when you are at a low point.

What is totally unacceptable is a teacher who seems to be permanently sour. Teachers who get to this state are jeopardising the education of their pupils. The joy of teaching seems to have disappeared for them and they should review their future because many children regard their lessons as downright awful. Such teachers have little respect for the pupils and set a poor example by being rude and bad tempered. They seem unapproachable and engender a climate of distrust in their classroom.

Delivery of lessons

One obvious source of behaviour problems can be the lesson and the quality of the teaching. A good lesson with appropriate activities can enthuse and inspire. A poorly thought-through lesson with activities that do not match the abilities of the pupils can switch them off.

Being a teacher is very demanding in many ways. To teach successfully requires a wide repertoire of skills. We should be secure in our knowledge of the subjects and how to teach each one. We need to know what each pupil is capable of and how they can be challenged. The activities should be varied to enable children with different learning styles to benefit. The delivery of the lesson must connect what has been learned with what comes next so that the class know where they are going. The teacher should activate their minds so they can take on new ideas and then demonstrate the application of them in a variety of contexts. Finally, the learning should be consolidated so that the children can recognise what they have learned and what they personally feel they need to do next (see Chapter 1: How do children learn?). Careful structuring of the learning taking all this into consideration is a complex and time-consuming task but it can yield surprising results.

Things do not always go smoothly and some teachers have difficulty working out how to teach some subjects, which can lead to ineffective lessons. This is not a failing. What is inexcusable is the failure to review why a lesson did not go well and then try to make improvements. Many teachers do this as a matter of course. You can usually tell when things have not gone well and your pupils will also give you some indication. Keeping the learning personal and alive for the children will minimise behaviour problems.

Low expectations

Classes of pupils are not homogeneous groups – there will be a spread of abilities. In many comprehensive schools this is likely to be quite wide, especially if there is a high proportion of children with learning difficulties. You could find you have the full ability range from Reception to Level 5. This is a daunting prospect because the planning of suitable activities to meet individual needs becomes a complicated task. Yet it can be achieved by organising the pupils into four groups: high, average, low ability and those with special needs who would benefit from being in a group of their own. Group composition will vary with subjects and should be organised using assessment data and individual education plans that you have. Current thinking also includes a 'wave' approach. Wave 1 – pupils who can make expected progress in the lesson. Wave 2 – pupils who could make progress if they were placed in groups with support. Wave 3 – pupils who are significantly delayed in their learning and need intensive support, possibly outside of some lessons.

Children are able to tell when a teacher has low expectations. They find the activities prosaic and easy, resulting in early completion. They soon realise they can get by with very little effort. Then the problems start because they have nothing to do. The unstructured time leads to behaviour issues. It is at those times that the teacher is under pressure because the children will distract those who are still working. Time invested in planning how to challenge the more able will reap dividends. The pupils will remain engaged and on-task, leaving you free to concentrate on managing the learning of all the pupils rather than helping some and dealing with the incidents of others.

Personalise the learning

Linking the learning to the personal experiences of the pupils will motivate them to engage more readily with it. Putting the idea or concept into a context will help the children understand why they are studying it. This can be quite difficult with some subjects, especially if the topic is an abstract one.

A very effective way of personalising something is to ask the children to empathise or role-play. Proposing questions like 'How would you feel if . . . ?', 'What would you do . . . ?', 'Can you think of another way that they could . . . ?' will bring the learning alive and let the pupils respond to it rather than treating them as empty vessels to be filled with facts.

We owe it to the pupils to look for ways that will help them get interested in the work, otherwise they will just switch off and cause trouble.

Boundaries

Children need boundaries to help them learn how to behave in different contexts. Problems can occur when the boundaries are absent or poorly defined. Teachers who have clear rules that are simple to follow and upheld in a fair and consistent way minimise problems.

Rules are put in place to protect the rights and feelings of the community. It is the responsibility of everyone to ensure they are adhered to (see Chapter 6: Values, beliefs and expectations). The adults in schools have a duty to establish the rules and children expect them to do this. Demonstrating that you are the leader and adult in the room is an essential part of ensuring that the children will behave. Once they know you are in charge they can relax and feel secure. Teachers who are not assertive and fail to establish a system of good order could end up with a troublesome class. The same can apply in the home. Parents who do not demonstrate their position allow their children to push back the boundaries and, ultimately, take control.

Seating

The way children are seated in a classroom can lead to problems. Allowing them to sit where they want will lead to small pockets of children who may have a tendency to be distracted. The solution is to work out a seating plan in advance. This requires knowledge of the friendship groups and the children who are likely to misbehave so that you can seat them appropriately. Some teachers favour a boy–girl arrangement but this can be uncomfortable for shy pupils.

There may be children in the group who have problems with their eyesight or hearing and need to be near the front. It may not be apparent at first but if you find a child is beginning to misbehave and/or their work is below standard, it is worth finding out whether this could be the reason.

Special needs

There are occasions when a class has a higher proportion of children with special needs. This is more likely in one-form-entry schools. It may be that they get identified only once they have been at the school for a number of years. Whatever the reason, it can be quite a challenge for a teacher and the behaviour of the class could be affected, leading to serious problems. If you find you are in this position you should discuss it with the Special Educational Needs Coordinator (SENCO) to decide how best to use the support. Make sure you have a clear behaviour code to ensure children understand what is expected of them.

Absence

The nature of planning curriculum subjects results in mini-programmes of work that focus on topics or key concepts. These may span a whole week for core subjects or a number of weeks for foundation subjects. Children who are absent could miss important lessons where new concepts are introduced. Then they find they do not understand what they are doing and fall behind everyone else. The teacher will endeavour to help the child but it is always harder to do once the rest of the class have moved on.

Children who are absent for short periods on a regular basis will experience this difficulty more often and it can create behavioural problems. Their feelings of being left out or in need of special attention single them out. They may resent the need for individual help or find they are waiting around for it and then get bored. Whatever the reason, the likelihood of an incident is increased, so teachers in this position need to take steps to avoid it.

Bullying

This is probably one of the darker sources of poor behaviour. It can be very difficult to detect and is often concealed by both the victim and the perpetrator. Behaviour that is out of keeping may be a sign that bullying is going on. A child may try to fit in with a particular peer group by doing things to impress them or copying their behaviour. Alternatively, a child being bullied may misbehave, either unwittingly or deliberately, to draw attention to themselves as a cry for help.

Bullying usually occurs when an individual or a group feel they are powerful and can force others to submit to them. It comes in many forms. It can be physical, verbal or territorial in the sense that the group isolates the victim and prevents them entering their circle or gang. Victims generally have something that singles them out as different. It may be a physical feature or an aspect of their personality. A child may have a need, such as wanting to be friends or to have someone to share their interests. The bully picks up on that need and exploits it. Children with learning difficulties are susceptible to being bullied because they are noticeable in schools by the support they get and the different work they may do.

All schools have their own ways of dealing with bullying, which can vary from sweeping it under the carpet and denying it is happening to some sophisticated approaches that include face-to-face interviews, restorative justice and strict contracts for change. The teacher's role is to be vigilant for the signs and act early when they think it is going on. Poor self-esteem is often at the root of bullying and can result in a child becoming vulnerable and a victim of bullying or even needing to bully others.

■ Redefining special needs

Rendall and Stuart (2005) suggest that special needs are not solely located within the child. They argue that there is a set of interrelated conditions involved which are located within the family and the school as well as the child. This view is very similar in many ways to the *Framework for the Assessment of Children in Need and their Families* mentioned earlier in this chapter.

All children have learning needs. The school system is set up in a way that allows the majority (those who could be described as having normal intellectual and physical development) to have their needs catered for through the curriculum designed for their year group. There are expected year group targets available from the Department for Education and Skills (DfES) on the Standards website (www.dfes.gov.uk). These clearly identify what children should be able to do in each subject by the end of any academic year. There will usually be a group of children who exceed these expectations in one or more subjects and who are described as 'gifted' or 'talented'. There will also be a group who do not reach the targets for their age in one or more subjects. A child who falls well below the expected levels in the core subjects is described as having special needs. In some cases the need is so profound that they have an educational statement. This is a legal document that details the strategies and the support the child is entitled to receive to enable them to meet the targets specified in it.

Identifying a need in an individual prompts a number of new questions. Does the child have difficulty in their learning that can be attributed to their cognitive development? Is it due to family circumstances or the strategies the school is using? When a child is underperforming, we need to interrogate what we do. We should consider whether changes could be made that might help. For example, if a child had behavioural difficulties and we changed our responses from rules and direct instructions to choices, would things be different?

We try to help pupils do their best by fostering a positive climate for learning and putting in place more opportunities for them to take responsibility for their own behaviour. In the next chapter, we will consider how the style you adopt as a teacher can obstruct or advance you towards this goal.

■ Review

Pupils may have a range of clinical reasons that will cause them to behave inappropriately.

NON-CLINICAL REASONS SUCH AS POOR SELF-ESTEEM, LACK OF BOUNDARIES OR MOTIVATION, PEER PRESSURE AND AN ABSENCE OF SELF-CONTROL MAY PREVENT A CHILD BEHAVING WELL.

Children will often try to blame others and we need to help them to recognise that if they were involved, they were making a choice.

Family dynamics may be a major reason for behavioural difficulties.

Significant numbers of troubled children have experienced a serious critical incident in their past.

Schools can have an impact on inappropriate behaviour, both in its cause and with helping children to modify it.

A teacher's style can be a factor in causing a child to misbehave.

Special needs are not always located within the child. The family and even the school may have 'special needs' that affect the way a child behaves.

Chapter 3
You are the expert

Classrooms are very busy places at times and it can be quite difficult maintaining an atmosphere of order where children feel free enough to take risks with their learning. The process of getting things organised or moving out to go to assembly or another room can quickly degenerate into an uncontrolled mêlée of little children all trying to do something slightly different at the same time. It is at moments like these that a style that is fair and consistent is needed to ensure that the classroom remains a productive place for learning.

You are the key resource in the classroom. You are more important than any other resource in the room because you know your pupils and how they work, what they enjoy and all their little foibles. You can adapt and change in a way that no other resource can. In short, you are invaluable.

When it comes to reading, you are the expert. You will know what you want each child to learn and how they will go about doing it. You will be able to model how you want them to read a text so they can pick up where to emphasise a word, pause between phrases and use intonation and accent to give the text light and shade. Teachers are the experts in all the subjects and that is what makes them such a unique force in the lives of their pupils.

You are also the expert in behaviour management in your room. Your own behaviour is their example to follow. Children will copy the behaviour of adults so it is crucial that you model how you want them to behave. You cannot expect the children to be told by you to do one thing when you are actually doing the opposite yourself. With this in mind, we will be looking at the styles teachers adopt in the classroom and the effects those styles have on the children.

Teachers are human beings and have their own particular expectations and ways of doing things. Some seem to manage behaviour effortlessly. In fact, to the uninformed observer it may seem that the children are always well behaved and incidents simply do not occur in the lessons. In stark contrast, a teacher may appear to be acting out the role of a slave galley overseer, striding around the classroom barking orders and cracking the whip. Why does this happen and just what is the best way of managing a class full of pupils? Some teachers believe they are directly responsible for the behaviour of their pupils and will be judged as failing if a pupil kicks off or they lose control of the class. The perception is that the teacher who has discipline problems is weak. Individual teachers who believe this will tend to use a range of strategies related to their personality. Some will appear successful because they are strong. They will be aggressive and overbearing. Those who try to use aggressive tactics but fail because they are weak eventually resort to appealing to the miscreants to stop. Their requests are ignored and the result is a total loss of control.

Occasionally you meet a teacher who seems to be naturally popular or charismatic. The children seem desperate to please because they like the teacher, but the problem is that they will not assume responsibility for their own behaviour. They are doing it to please the teacher, not for themselves. When that teacher is away they may not feel any obligation to behave for the substitute teacher.

All of these styles are reactive to the situations. They do not enable the pupils to actively develop a responsibility for their own behaviour. Choices are not offered and a programme for development is often absent. The teachers expect the children to behave and when they don't they react in an erratic way. So let's look more closely at the different reactive styles.

The aggressive style

Julia had believed teachers should have strict control over the pupils. Classrooms were places of order, quiet and work. No one was allowed to talk unless they put up their hand. Silence and uniformity were the benchmarks of a well-behaved class and therefore a good teacher.

Julia came to England two years ago and started work as a supply teacher. She liked it so much she decided to get a more permanent position and eventually managed to secure one in a London school. She was given a Year 4 class and set about establishing herself by imposing a strict regime. At first, other staff and parents were very impressed because she was not going to have any messing about. They thought the children would have a good experience with her. Unfortunately, this was not going to be the case.

The weeks passed and it became evident that something was wrong in her room. It came to a head when Dan exploded, kicked over a chair and stormed out of the room. He made for the hall, followed by the learning support assistant. He refused to listen to her and when she tried to get nearer he picked up a chair and threw it at her. Then he climbed up the wall bars and stayed put despite the efforts of the Head and Deputy. In the end, the Head decided to exclude him and his mum had to come to the school and collect him.

So what went wrong for Dan?

Amy, the behaviour support adviser, was called to observe Dan in the class to get to the bottom of the problem. She was experienced and had seen many teachers in action. After several sessions she came to the conclusion that the children seemed unnaturally quiet. They appeared to be keeping their heads down. They didn't volunteer much in the lesson and seemed to lack any enthusiasm for what they were doing.

Children will make mistakes and learn from them if they are handled well. Amy felt that Julia reacted unfairly and inconsistently to any kind of behaviour that did not conform to her expectations. For example, if a child blurted out the answer to a question she would come down heavily on them with a load of verbal reprimands and a punishment that was clearly way over the top. This was probably what happened with Dan because a similar incident occurred when Amy was observing him.

Another pupil called Billy turned round to ask a girl behind him if he could borrow the dictionary. Julia spotted it and shouted at him to keep his eyes on his own work. Then she told him he would lose his break for that. Well, Billy couldn't cope. After all, he was only asking for a book; it was not like he was doing anything really bad and now he was getting punished. He looked forward to his breaks – he liked to play football and couldn't wait to get out and meet up with his mates and get a game going. The whole thing was too much for him. He stood up, pushed his books off the table and went for the door. Julia ordered him to stop but he didn't take any notice. He was gone. What was obvious to Amy was the way the rest of the class were behaving. They seemed to be scared out of their minds. They were quiet as mice. Many were cowering and staring at the floor.

What to look for

The aggressive teacher rarely coaches the pupils in how to behave. They take sole responsibility for the behaviour of the class. They believe that a good teacher has complete control and commands respect by establishing a climate of fear and oppression. After a while the pupils are like robots, doing exactly what they are told. They are not involved in any decision about the rules. The teacher orders them about and they are expected to obey. They stray at their peril!

The teacher believes in rigid, unquestioned authority and expects all pupils to behave. There are usually quite a few consequences given out but rarely, if ever, are rewards given. Some aggressive teachers will even go as far as describing the school as a battleground and their methods as 'guerrilla tactics' in a bid for survival. They believe they have the right to get what they want and have no time for pupil rights. They do not respect their pupils and use derogatory terms to describe them e.g.:

I'll get those little buggers to behave if it is the last thing I do!

It is not surprising that teachers who think like this end up being disliked by their pupils and have more than their fair share of incidents in the classroom. If you model aggressive, oppressive, disdainful, bullying behaviour, the children end up copying it. They have little else to choose from.

What happens when the pupils have had enough?

Once, they would probably have accepted it. Teachers used to have a different status and discipline systems in schools were punitive. Today things are different. Children with enough courage or insufficient fear will answer back and end up in a conflict because aggressive teachers do not expect them to question their authority. When this happens it becomes a battle of wills that the aggressive teacher must win at all costs. Losing would result in a loss of face. What inevitably happens is the teacher focuses on the child's secondary behaviour and uses it to suppress and gain a victory.

Case Study

Adil and Jordan were chatting about the experiment they were doing in Science. They were unaware that they were getting animated and speaking loudly. Ruth did not like their lack of respect. She had told them to do the experiment and record the results quietly. She expected them to know what she meant by 'quiet'.

'I said you must work quietly. You two do not seem to know the meaning of quietly!'

'But we were talking about the results Miss!'

Ruth got annoyed that a pupil would dare to answer back in her class.

'Don't be so cheeky. You always seem to be making a noise Adil.'

'But I . . .'

'That's enough. Do not answer back. Leave the room. I will deal with you later.'

The teacher turned a small thing into a serious incident because she felt the pupil was being rude and cheeky. She used a major consequence for a minor incident. Children will talk and if they are interested they will often forget themselves and get carried away in the excitement, which is a good thing if you think about it. We want the children to be interested in the work so that they are motivated. Ruth was put out by their attempts to justify their raised voices. She got entangled in the secondary behaviour and ended up escalating the incident by responding to it.

The aggressive teacher regards the children as the weak underdogs and will not give them a way out of a difficult situation to help them save face. They must be kept in their place and respect the teacher's authority.

The long-term effects

Children who find themselves in an oppressive regime will not grow in stature. They will keep their heads down in order to stay out of trouble and avoid getting noticed. When they are in trouble they feel they are the victims. They have no way out; no chance to redeem themselves and end up being humiliated. This will damage their self-esteem and any relationship between teacher and pupils will deteriorate.

Respect will disappear from the room and incidents will increase. Individual children will become the targets as the teacher tries to contain them. Bullying may develop among the children as they adopt the behaviour the teacher is modelling in order to vent their negative feelings of frustration. The teacher will look to blame everybody but herself for the poor behaviour. The children end up regarding the teacher as the enemy.

They start to cheat, lie and make excuses in order to pass the blame when the teacher picks on them. They feign illness and devise intricate schemes to get out of lessons. Loyalties and trust among friends may also be replaced by personal survival instincts. Eventually they will vent their anxieties on each other.

Children can be turned off school when there is a climate of fear pervading the classroom. They will go home and tell their parents stories about the teacher and incidents that occurred. This will set the parents against the teacher as they will side with their children and make things worse. The end result will be a lack of trust and calm in the room.

▪ The passive style

This is the opposite to the aggressive style. The teacher will be uncertain of their role as the leader in the classroom. She lacks the belief that she can manage the pupils and believes that others are much better at it, especially extrovert teachers. She will feel helpless to change and does not think she is in the same league as her colleagues. She will underestimate her abilities and describe more successful teachers as gifted because of their innate ability. Her insecurity will eventually be picked up by the pupils through her efforts to be liked as a person rather than for her teaching. She will seek recognition and satisfaction by backing away from unpopular decisions, confrontations and challenging pupils.

The passive teacher is characterised by efforts to be popular that include ingratiating herself. She will have fragile feelings and will take criticism badly. She will plan her lessons in great detail but is not a forward planner in terms of managing the behaviour of her class. She ends up having to react to incidents and usually does it badly because she has not worked out her responses.

Some teachers can be very sharp and on the look-out for even the slightest problem. The passive teacher does not possess this awareness and can often be oblivious to conflicts going on in her class. It may be that she is afraid and blanks them out. Remaining aloof helps prevent her from becoming unpopular but her abdication of responsibility actually adds to the problem. Once some children get away with things without being challenged, the door is opened for them to push back the boundaries. They will lose touch with what is acceptable and get confused. In order to find out what they can and cannot do they have to continue to test the teacher and so the number of incidents increases. The passive teacher is put under even more pressure and starts to feel that all she is doing is 'putting out fires'. She starts to become wary and questions her reasons for becoming a teacher. She used to think that the pupils should respect her but she has done little to command that respect.

 Case Study

The door was open and any passer-by who looked in could see that this was no normal classroom. The desks were not in orderly arrangements, a number of chairs had been pushed haphazardly together and there were some pens and erasers and pieces of paper on the carpet. The cloakroom area was more like a jumble sale, with jackets and coats piled onto pegs or laying on the floor where they had been dumped. The class had just left the room to go out to play and if it had been possible to rewind the film to see what had been the cause of the untidiness, this is what you would have seen.

The Year 5 class were getting restless with ten minutes to go before playtime. The Maths lesson had dragged on for most of them. They were supposed to be solving problems but the problem most of the children had was with their teacher. The work Maria set them was certainly on the Year Plan but a considerable number of the children were finding it hard. Her explanations and examples had been punctuated with interruptions and disruptions from pupils who had grown impatient with her. They spent most of the time messing around, annoying each other and causing a nuisance, and Maria seemed incapable of doing anything about it. Her interventions were of the pleading kind. For example:

'Come on now John, please stop talking and get on with your work.'

'Mark, if only you would leave those blinds alone you could get on and do this work.'

'I really want you all to quieten down. It is not fair on the class next door.'

None of her requests appeared to have any effect and most of the class seemed unable to stop themselves. It had not always been like this. The first half of the autumn term had been okay. Things gradually deteriorated as the weeks went by and the children realised that Maria was not setting firm boundaries. She was not a very confident person but she wanted to be a teacher because she liked the idea of helping young people. Her previous classes had been well behaved but that was probably because they were younger and did not feel they needed to challenge her. But now, faced with a more difficult class, she realised she wasn't managing very well.

The lessons before break and home time usually ended in chaos. The children would hear the bell signalling the end of the lesson and would start getting ready to go. Maria had tried to do it in an orderly way but she never seemed to see it through. One child would get up out of turn and Maria would try to get them to sit down but they would ignore her. They would say things like:

'I'm just getting my coat Miss,'

and continue what they were doing. Maria's reply would be:

'Well hurry up and then sit down because it's not your turn.'

Allowing one child to get away with it signalled to the others to follow. In the end she just gave up and let them do it their way. This became the trend throughout the whole day and Maria felt impotent to reverse it. The more sensible children would go home and tell their parents about things that had happened, which started to worry them. They began talking at the school gate and the rumours quickly spread. Maria felt she was losing it and grew more and more unhappy.

The passive teacher is timid and shrew-like. She will say things that show she lacks any real status and belief in her position as the adult in charge. She will try to persuade or even plead with children rather than direct them. Her attempts will come over as lacking any authority. Her body language will reinforce her lack of authority. She will often appear tired and defeated. She will have a resigned expression, begin to stoop, have rounded shoulders and possibly even look like she is cowering at times. The overall image is of someone who sees themselves as a victim and feels defeated. She is taking it all personally and this is what the teacher should not do. Everyone is responsible for their own behaviour and your guard against being drawn into this style lies in that belief.

The passive teacher who believes she is responsible will become preoccupied, questioning her ability. She will be filled with self-doubt, become isolated and emotionally drained. She will start to lose the ability to act fairly and will appear erratic. She will get angry and then find herself feeling guilty because she has overreacted. When she tries to reverse what is happening she gets bogged down in secondary issues.

What happens when a passive teacher starts to lose it?

A growing resentment builds up between the teacher and the pupils. She starts to dislike them rather than their behaviour. The children become confused about what they can and cannot do and resent the teacher for being weak. The better-behaved pupils feel they are getting a raw deal and see the naughty children getting away with things. They may do one of two things – either see it as a bit of fun and join in or try to get help with their work but grow frustrated because the teacher never seems to have time for them. The disruptive children monopolise the teacher's time and the only way for the other children to get attention is to be naughty as well.

The teacher will eventually give up using the behaviour code, as it does not seem to work for her. She uses the rewards as bribes to get the disruptive children back on-task. Then children who are behaving feel they are being ignored. This style does not help children make choices. It confuses them and prevents them from developing internal checks. In the end the teacher retreats from the recognised approaches, fails to help the pupils and becomes more stressed, which results in patchy attendance and negative feelings about teaching.

The proactive style

This style is the one to develop, as it will give you the skills and confidence to do your job well. It will also enable your pupils to become more independent and responsible for their own learning, actions and behaviour. The proactive teacher is assertive and works at making sure she gets what she wants in her classroom. She is confident about her skills and develops a climate of respect based on the rights and responsibilities of both children and adults.

She believes that a safe, secure environment will contribute to a positive atmosphere where all the children will feel valued and will appreciate the support and friendship of the others in the class. She is clear about her expectations and communicates them using unambiguous directions. She backs up what she says and wants with her actions. Pupils who follow directions and do well are praised. Those who test or defy are challenged.

The underlying foundation for everything she does is that every pupil can succeed if they try. She knows that success can look different for each child and recognises it when she sees them making progress. Equally, when things become difficult she offers support and encouragement to let the children know she is helping them. She does not chastise children who make mistakes. Instead she helps them see where they went wrong, why and how they can overcome their barrier and move on. When a child makes a mistake she does not take it personally and she does not become emotionally involved.

The proactive teacher believes in her right to teach and asserts that right whenever necessary. She does not need to shout. She remains calm and redirects the child using clear, fair rules backed up with pre-agreed rewards and consequences to keep the pupils on-task.

Case Study

Beebee wanted all of her pupils to do well. She modelled her approach on that of a sports coach. She built the kids up, showed them what success looked like and how to get it, then convinced them they could do it because she believed they could. Her classroom was a positive one. Of course, she had the usual problems any teacher encounters, such as children who bicker over small things, scrapes and arguments at playtimes and the occasional disruption during lessons. The difference was the way she handled them. There was an air of respect in the way she talked to the children. She didn't overdo the 'fluffy' kindness. She showed she cared but preferred to get into chats about the interesting things the children were doing with her at school or at home in their spare time. When things went well she let the children know and showed her appreciation. When things went wrong she intervened judiciously and fairly, using just the right amount of disapproval without getting angry. Her strength was in recognising when a child was making an extra effort, often after they had made a mistake.

An example of this was the way she helped Matt, who had really been going through a difficult phase. He had been having a lot of problems at home with his mum. His dad had left and he was probably unable to come to terms with it. He started to get physical when his friends wouldn't play with him. That just drove them further away. He desperately wanted friends and wanted to play football during breaks. It got to a point where he didn't seem to have anyone. He had bullied so many of the children in his class that they didn't want to know. He turned to food for comfort. His teacher found him very hard to manage. He began to get quite disruptive in the class. The slightest thing upset him and he would go for the other child. His mum was always getting called to the school to talk to him but that didn't have much effect.

The Head Teacher called a meeting to discuss strategies with the SENCO, his mum, his teacher and the Key Stage Leader. If they didn't get something in place soon he would be heading for exclusion. They decided to move him across to another class in his year group. Beebee was the teacher and the SENCO felt she might be able to manage his behaviour because she had been quite successful with another child with similar behaviour last year. She agreed, so Matt moved classes.

He had become so used to children saying they didn't want him around and the teacher telling him she was fed up with him that he was really surprised when he met Beebee. She greeted him warmly and told him she was really looking forward to having him in her class. The other children welcomed him and didn't seem to be afraid. At the end of the first day he went home and told his mum how much he liked his new teacher and that he had played football with his new friends.

Matt didn't really need much, just people being positive about him. When he did something well Beebee praised him and he seemed to swell with pride – he really responded very well every time she gave him some. When he didn't follow directions she intervened in a calm but firm way, using her three-step system that allowed him time to think about his behaviour.

The changes seemed to happen within a short space of time. It is not always possible or desirable to move children from one class to another. It unsettles them, takes them away from their friends and may even affect their self-esteem if they are put in a class a year above and end up being one of the least able. In Matt's case, his friends were turning their backs on him. The teacher and support assistant had started being very negative towards Matt and his mother was finding the comments about him at the school gate were starting to get to her. So all in all, it was a good move. The fresh start helped him feel more positive about himself.

Beebee talked to his mum about his diet because he had grown significantly and was overweight. Matt wanted to go swimming with his new class and had become aware of his appearance, so with his mum's help he started 'getting into shape' as he called it. He took up cycling and they cut out the junk food at home. It is early days so you couldn't say things are back to normal yet, but Matt seems a lot happier. He is still overweight but he's got friends who accept him and he doesn't bully them. He is really quite mixed up about his dad although he doesn't seem to be blaming his mum so much. But what seems to have made the most impact were the comments that Beebee made right at the start about wanting him in her class and liking him.

The assertive teacher uses a wide repertoire of strategies to show she is in charge and gets what she wants. It is not just what she says but how she says it. She does not stand in a confrontational way with her arms folded, glaring, pouting or wagging her finger in the face of a child. She does not get right up close and shout in a child's face. She respects their personal space. She adopts an open and relaxed posture and smiles even when the child seems angry or confrontational. The level of her voice drops as the pupil raises his voice and her tone is warm and friendly in order to bring back calm to the situation. She holds the child with direct eye contact and uses humour to defuse things.

What to aim for

The proactive teaching style can be achieved but needs to be worked on and practised. It is not a gift or an innate ability and much of this book is about developing the skills of this style. The proactive teacher has presence in the room. She shows she is in charge and organised by being smartly dressed, well groomed and decisive in her actions. The room reflects this by being tidy with well-labelled resources, stimulating displays and a sense of fun running through.

She cultivates a culture of respect for the rights of each individual and defends them so the children feel safe, secure and able to learn. (The children are not in control – that is not the style of the proactive teacher.) She guides and supports them so they can take responsibility for their own behaviour. She values them as people and lets them know it. She uses measured responses and when in doubt will seek advice. In short, the children know exactly what to expect from the teacher and how they should behave.

Teachers define the atmosphere in the classroom with the style they adopt.

Styles can be reactive or responsive.

Reactive teachers do not plan ahead, they respond aggressively or passively.

Proactive teachers plan for good behaviour and manage assertively.

STYLES of TEACHER

Proactive teachers assert their right to teach as the leader in the room.

They show they respect the pupils and command respect in return.

The proactive style is not a gift. It is achieved through practice.

The proactive teacher remains calm, fair and consistent.

Chapter 4

It's not what you say but the way that you say it

The way we talk to children as well as what we say will help them make up their minds about us. A positive climate for learning is something worth working for because of the advantages it brings. Therefore, we need to consider the tone and inflexion of our voices together with what we say if we are to maximise our chances of securing that climate. Teachers who lack enthusiasm tarnish the children's opinions about us all. The routine diet of 'Blah, Blah, Blah, drone, drone' together with barked orders and wining, nagging criticism would be enough to turn anyone off and there is no reason for it.

Thankfully, not every teacher is like that. There are a significant majority who enjoy their job, gain enormous satisfaction when they see children progressing and really care about what they do. Their enthusiasm and dedication rub off and the pupils like them. They are the ones who produce a positive climate – so how do they do it? What do they do that is so different? In the last chapter we looked at how a teacher's style can affect the children and in this chapter we will look at how teachers can use their voice as a powerful tool. They will employ many of the following to help them in their work:

- adopt a positive attitude;

- consider their delivery;

- agree and acknowledge;

- plan their responses;

■ use humour;

■ use controlled anger;

■ offer praise and encouragement;

■ make their praise specific;

■ model good manners;

■ utilise the 'goal disclosure technique'.

Your voice as a tool

Our voice is a powerful tool so it is worth learning how to get the most from it. Voices can reveal and influence. The stalwart words of Winston Churchill and the stirring speeches of Martin Luther King moved millions to join them in their pursuit of freedom. Equally, the manic rantings of Adolf Hitler persuaded a whole generation of German people to follow him. Anger, fear and humour can all be communicated by using different tones of voice. Aggressive or disruptive pupils can be pushed further away or brought under control depending on how we speak to them. The passive teacher will be uncertain or even frightened and her voice will falter and be quieter than the aggressive teacher who shouts and bellows orders. In contrast, the assertive teacher will have a repertoire of styles for different occasions – loud to gain attention, soft to calm anger and business-like to get things done. Try practising controlling your voice to achieve these results.

Teachers are well known for their ability to talk at length. Many have the gift of being able to speak clearly and with considered annunciation. There are some who feel they need to speak loudly to ensure every child will hear them, but this is unnecessary. All the children in the room will be able to hear you quite easily when you speak in a normal voice if they are actually listening, so there is no need to shout. The reason that some teachers raise their voices on occasions is because the class is not silent. Getting silence is one of the most important requirements, together with being able to keep all the children in their seats. Once you achieve these you will have control. There are a number of ways of getting silence in primary schools and these are explained below.

The sound signal

You can use a bell, whistle, triangle or short burst of music to signal to the class that it is time to stop what they are doing, look your way and pay attention. Rewarding the fastest pupil or table can encourage them to speed up.

Targeted commands

This is a great way of bringing the whole class together by giving them a series of commands that they all follow. You will need to train them in advance so they will all know what to do. Your commands can vary but the procedure will remain the same. It begins with a signal to grab attention, then the teacher directs.

'Heads' – the pupils touch their head with both hands.

'Shoulders' – then they touch their shoulders with both hands.

'Arms' – they finish by folding their arms and sitting silently.

Variations can include '3, 2, 1 . . . Freeze!' (or blow a whistle). The children must freeze as statues. This is good during physical activities such as playtimes and PE.

Time target

Children like a challenge and this one is against the clock. You will need a visual timer such as a large clock with a second hand or a minute sand timer. When you are ready to change activities tell the children to pack up and sit down with their arms folded and watch the timer in silence.

The rhythm change

This is a good one for the beginnings and endings of lessons. It is also a very good activity for use in a brain gym session (see Chapter 1: How do children learn?). The children will be engaged in tasks. You clap your hands twice quite loudly and then pause. Your expression should be an expectant one which is saying, 'Come on then, what's next?' The children may look puzzled but the usual response will be copy and clap twice. Wait a few moments and if they do not copy you, repeat and give them an open, playful look of 'This is fun, why don't you give it a try?' Whatever you do, do not say anything. Once they have the idea and have clapped, click your fingers twice. The whole class will eventually join in. Build up a rhythm that they can copy. Then introduce a call and response that they will know. For example, DA, DE-DE, DA DA and the pupils reply with DA DA. Try varying the speed and end up with the pupils giving their reply. They will be waiting for your next move . . . and you have them. They will be giving you their attention.

The hand up
This is used to stop children when they are engaged in an activity. Raise your arm. The children are taught that when they see you or another pupil raise an arm, they copy. Eventually they will all have their arms up, showing they are ready for you.

The passive concert
Teach your pupils how to participate in and make the most of the class 'passive concert'. The children close their eyes, rest their hands on the table and listen as you review the main points of the lesson with quiet music playing in the background. This is usually done near the end of the lesson but it can also be used for reading them a story.

The quality audience
Discuss and agree the directions for this procedure with the whole class and publish them as an A3 laminated display. The routine for a quality audience is very simple:

- Announce to the class, 'Can I have a quality audience in five seconds please – 5, 4, 3, 2, 1.'
- At the end of the countdown, announce 'Quality audience, now please'.
- Hold up your hand or an object to reinforce this and assert your request for a quality audience (which should be silence).

(After Smith, A., Lovatt, M. and Wise, D. 2003)

The very noisy class

There is one particular method of getting silence that is very effective if you do not know the children. Supply teachers will find this particularly useful.

Case Study

Natalie was an agency teacher. She had been sent to a primary school in East London. The class was Year 5 and the teacher had been off for several weeks. The school had been unable to find a replacement so the class had had a stream of different teachers. This was having a detrimental effect on them and especially on their behaviour. As Natalie approached the room she could hear the racket through the open door. Suddenly a boy appeared, took one look at her and darted back into the room. Natalie went in and could see from the sight that met her eyes that this was going to be a hard day. She walked confidently to the front of the room. The noise continued as most of the class ignored her. They had got used to teachers with little or no authority. Natalie looked straight at a group who had glanced up to check out who they had been given for the day.

'Raise your hand if you can hear what I am saying,' Natalie said in a voice that was just loud enough for this group to catch but not for any of the others. All the children in the group and one or two others nearby put up their hands. She acknowledged them with a smile and repeated, shifting her attention to another group. They joined the first group by putting up their hands. She soon had the whole class looking at her. She put one finger to her lips and made a sign for silence, then told them to put their hands down because she had something important to say. She had gained control and kept calm in the process. Furthermore, she hadn't needed to shout.

Keeping silence with infants

Little children can be very enthusiastic about school and changes during their day. Using the same system for all ages may not always work. One powerful way of getting children to do what you want is to utilise their imagination.

Steve started with the school in September and was given the Year 1 class. He had never taken such young ones so he needed to change the ways he worked with them. He had watched a colleague in his previous school who had developed a very effective way of getting all the children in the class to listen attentively and always do what he asked.

Steve went out at the weekend and got himself a cute little soft toy. It was a cat with a sad, endearing expression. On Monday he got his class to sit and told them a story about how he was walking along a road in the middle of nowhere when he came across a cat. The cat followed him and every time he stopped and looked back the cat sat down and looked back at him. He walked on for about a mile and still the cat followed him and sat down every time he stopped. There were no houses around and he thought the cat must be a stray. Eventually he stopped and gave the cat a bit of his lunch. It ate it eagerly and was obviously very hungry. Then it hopped up on to his lap, curled round and flopped down, purring loudly. Steve stroked it and tickled its ear. It closed its eyes and leaned against his hand, obviously enjoying the contact. When it was time to go, Steve stood up and the cat leapt to the ground but did not wander off. He felt he could not leave the poor little pussycat so he picked it up and tucked it inside his jacket where it purred happily.

Steve took the cat home with him and looked after it. The one thing the cat did not like was noise so whenever anyone came round to his house and spoke loudly it went and hid. Steve realised this and asked his visitors to whisper. Once they had lowered their voices, the cat came out and joined them.

When he had finished his story, Steve asked the children whether they would like to meet his cat. He told them its name and reminded them that they must always whisper or talk quietly when it was around. He got them all to promise because he didn't want his cat to be frightened by them. Then he brought out the cat.

Every time he wanted silence or quiet he would bring out the cat. Steve would often be seen walking in front of his class down the corridor or filing into assembly holding his cat. The children were absolutely quiet. They were captivated by the story and immersed themselves in it.

Insisting on attention

It is pointless trying to begin teaching if the class are not giving you their full attention. If you let disruptions go unchallenged and push on to try to teach, you will have shown the pupils that it doesn't matter if they are not paying attention. Teachers do this at their peril and it is often the first step on the road to a challenging class. So, when you are ready to start, get their attention before you begin by saying, 'Good morning'. This can be hard work and can take as long as five minutes, but it is essential.

You may need to be much more direct if you have a lot of pupils in the class who are not responding to any of these strategies. Stand at the front of the room and wait for a break between the chatting, calling out etc., then address the most disruptive children. 'Guys, hands up if you have anything to say or share with the class.' The children may ignore you at first so repeat and keep at it until they do what you ask, then briefly thank them and move on. If necessary, wait and continue directing with phrases like:

'Eyes and ears this way.'

'Listening with your ears and eyes.'

'Hands up if you have anything to share with the class.'

These are all positive directions and will get your class calm and settled. Never use a question or appear to be pleading, e.g.:

'Please be quiet.'

'Please will you put your hand up.'

Simple directions given assertively will work, but questions result in unnecessary responses. When you finally have their attention, thank them and say 'Good morning/afternoon'.

◼ **Be positive**

I was in school and had the opportunity to speak to a number of groups of children about the way teachers talked. They made the following comments that are very revealing:

'They are too bossy, always telling us to do this and do that!'

'I'm always being told to be quiet.'

'They say, don't do this or don't do that!'

'I never get to do anything. I'm told I can't do it . . . not now!'

'They say, "Stop talking!"'

It seems all terribly negative and hardly conducive to a good climate for learning. Children who can remember only these kinds of comments are probably not getting much in the way of positive reinforcement. This needs to be reversed and the best way is to model positive language for your pupils. Rephrase negatives as positive, affirmative directions. Turn 'Don'ts' into 'Dos'.

'Don't run' becomes 'Walk quietly please'. 'Don't forget to put your chair away' contains a double negative, 'don't' and 'forget'. Turned around, it becomes 'Remember to put your chairs under the tables'.

Try to turn directions into fun activities. 'I don't want to find any more books left out' can become 'Let's see if we can beat the clock'. (Then invert the sand timer.) 'Okay, go.' 'Don't all call out at once' becomes 'Hands up' or 'One at a time please'.

Some difficult situations can be dealt with by asking direct questions instead of telling the child off. For example: 'Omar, can you tell me what the Romans might have thought about our weather?' This is far better than 'Stop talking while I am speaking Omar. You are very rude and I am sick of having you muttering while I am trying to teach!'

The question refocuses the child on the lesson and prevents the flow from being disrupted. Note the question requires the child to empathise and use his imagination. Factual questions demand accuracy and may embarrass the child because he may not have been listening.

Consider the delivery

Listen to great politicians and ask yourself what it is that makes them such good speakers. There is something in the way they deliver their speeches that holds attention. Good comedians do it as well. The well-known Irish comedian, the late Dave Allen, was a master of delivery – his stories would hold audiences until the punch line. We can learn a great deal from the way performers and politicians entertain and persuade.

A technique that is extremely effective is the well-timed pause or delay. This can be useful when you are trying to get the attention of the class. The children are chatting or engaged in a discussion activity. The teacher either calls the pupil's name or gives a direction: 'Right, look this way . . . (pause)'.

They wait and hold everyone's attention momentarily, then deliver the rest of the direction: '. . . close your textbooks and be ready for a quiz'.

It is important to speak confidently and assertively and to act as if you expect the class to do as you say.

Many teachers fall into the same trap and try to give directions before they have got the full attention of the class. They end up having to shout over the din of bags being opened, books being taken out and put away or children just not listening because the teacher never waits for them to be quiet. When they do eventually try to hear the instructions they realise they have missed something and have to ask another pupil, which adds to the background noise. The teacher is aware that they have not heard and tries to repeat the instructions until the whole thing turns into a farce.

Give clear, concise, simple instructions and do not move on until everyone has heard.

This is done by gauging how much your pupils can process at once and then breaking down your directions so that they are simple to follow.

> *'Stop work, arms folded and facing the front.'*

This will bring the class to attention and most will fall silent. Address the ones who are still talking by name.

> *'Ahmed . . . (pause) . . . facing the front and listening thanks.'*

Thanking the child is a way of showing you assume they will do as you ask. Once everyone is attending, move on to the next direction.

> *'Green table, collect in the scissors please.'*

Important directions like reminding the children about arrangements for a school trip should not be left until the end of the day. Children become unsettled during endings so it is best to leave time in the middle of a lesson (see Chapter 1: How do children learn?).

▪ Agree and acknowledge

Schools are complex organisations with many rules, restrictions and procedures that children are expected to follow. It is not surprising to hear them asking questions in order to make sense of it all. Sometimes they will be unsure about something and will ask permission. In our efforts to develop a positive climate, we may inadvertently deal with these little requests in a negative way that sends out the wrong message. For example:

> *'Can I get my lunch box?'*

> *'No, it's not your turn.'*

The reply could easily be rephrased and turned into a more positive and helpful response simply by changing it from a negative reprimand into a direction.

> *'Yes, when the Red Tribe are all sitting, your group can get their lunch boxes.'*

Partially agreeing with the child shows you are seeing it from their point of view and helps you become part of their world. It is a useful tactic in defusing difficult situations and avoiding any escalation of conflict, especially with children who are emotionally vulnerable or have low self-esteem. They can be more effectively helped when you frame your comments in a positive way. Statements like 'Don't shout out like that!' can be changed to 'Remember, hands up if you want to say something.'

> 'Don't come in here swearing and cussing like that!' becomes 'I can see you are upset, let me settle the class and then we can talk about it.'

> 'You're late. I am fed up with the way you drift in after everyone else!' becomes 'Hello, you are five minutes late. Are you okay? If you go and sit down I will be with you in a minute.'

> 'Stop whining. I can't understand a word you are saying,' can be changed to 'Katy, I can see you have a problem. Just take a moment to collect your thoughts. Now, tell me how I can help.'

The most important thing to remember is to not become emotionally involved. The child will react to your feelings, so if you are calm and patient they will calm down too. Acknowledge their feelings in your opening words, then redirect. With more serious incidents you may need to calm the class as well. Quietly check that they know what they are doing and have got everything they need before going back to the child to deal with their problem. Keep things moving and match your response to the disruption, ensuring that your intervention is in proportion and as minimal as possible.

Avoid getting drawn into meaningless conversations and stick to the point. Keep focused on what the class should be doing. You will probably get comments like 'This is boring. Why can't we go on the computer?' Refrain from getting annoyed. Remember, the child may genuinely be finding the work boring. Partially agree with them because that goes a long way in turning things around. Maybe you could even inject some humour.

'This work is dull!' 'Can I see? (The teacher looks at the textbook or worksheet for a few seconds) . . . Yes you are right,' (with a smile, agreeing).

She then redirects and makes an offer of help.

'. . . but this is the work we are doing today (redirecting). Would you like some help getting started?' (rebuilding).

Sometimes a child will object to the work for other reasons. 'I'm not doing this. I did this stuff yesterday!'

It is easy to respond and I have seen some teachers do it quite insensitively. 'Yes, hardly anyone got it right. You didn't get it so I am having to go over it all again,' (she sighs and looks up to the ceiling with an incredulous expression).

This response will not resolve things. All the teacher is doing is venting her frustration. In reality it could be that she was expecting too much from the children. A far more positive approach would go like this: 'Yes, we did, didn't we . . . (agreeing with the pupil) . . . so you should be able to do it now . . . (redirecting) . . . Do you need any help with it?' (rebuilding).

▧ **Planned responses**

We probably all have our fair share of bad days when things do not go well. We may be tired, not in the best of health or perhaps something has not gone right at home. It is on these days that we do not cope as well. We get over-emotional about things, our tolerance levels go down and we end up getting upset, frustrated, annoyed, sad or anxious. Our ability to respond rationally becomes impaired as we act out our feelings. Our heart tends to rule our mind and on these days we will express our feelings with comments like 'That class really got on my nerves,' or 'I can't take much more of that today.'

We may target particular children: 'David is really trying my patience.' 'I'm going to swing for him if he carries on like that.' It is at times like this that we need a response plan. Such a plan can be useful for the day-to-day niggling, low-level disruptions as well as the more serious incidents.

Most teachers will probably be in the habit of producing detailed plans for lessons, but have you ever considered planning for good behaviour? What we are talking about here are the actual strategies that you will use as well as the code of rules, rewards and consequences. Your plan will enable you to work out how you will address the behaviour in the least intrusive way. The sorts of disruptions that you may need a plan for include:

- a pupil arriving late;

- not wearing the correct school uniform;

- calling out;

- being out of the seat;

- forgetting PE kit or bringing in toys etc.;

- little quarrels and name-calling.

You need to decide when and how you will use your new skills to help develop a positive climate for learning so the whole class can move forward as a learning community.

The underlying rule to remember is to remain calm. That does not mean to chill out or not be vigilant. There is a balance between being assertive as the leading adult in the room while communicating a feeling of being calm and in control. It is a skill that can be learned. So where do we start?

Do not react to the behaviour

It is easy to get annoyed or jump in too quickly without knowing what to do. If need be, take time to think. Allowing yourself to get angry will simply fuel the situation and whip up the children. You may be drawn into the secondary behaviour and then the child who is looking for a response will have the advantage, so step back and calm yourself first.

Case Study

A child had been talking, getting up and down, fiddling, tapping and eventually she annoyed another girl. The teacher had been trying to keep her on-task but without success.

The unplanned, emotional response

'That's it, I've had enough of your constant disruption. No matter what I say, you seem to be dead set on ignoring me. Well, you can get out and go to the Head. I don't want you in this room any more!'

The teacher over-reacted and used a major consequence for a minor incident. She did not stop to think. She made it personal by saying 'I've had enough' and then she passed on the problem too quickly. What will she do when she gets a far more serious incident to deal with?

The planned, rational response

'Sabrina, I have given you several warnings about being off-task and you have chosen to ignore them so I want you to collect your things and move to (this) table for five minutes. Show me that you can do your work quietly and I will let you return to your place.'

The teacher has remained calm and followed through after the warnings which is vital if the children are to learn that you mean what you say. She used phrases that she had worked out in advance together with a pre-planned consequence that the whole class knew about. Her rational response gave Sabrina an opportunity to take ownership of her behaviour by having a choice. She also allowed her an opportunity to try again once the consequence was served.

Internal exclusions from the class should not be used lightly. They should come when all the other alternatives have been exhausted. In this example, the pupil may repeat her behaviour later in the lesson, in which case the same response would be used. If after three or four more similar incidents it looks like the child may have a specific difficulty, then a meeting should be called with colleagues and the parent/carer to find a new strategy.

It is important to limit the response to the behaviour that matters. All too often, teachers feel they need to deal with everything that occurs and they are right in some respects. Children who break a rule or prevent others from learning do need correcting, but the intervention needs to be as unintrusive as possible. Picking up things like inappropriate uniform, lateness, calling out and all the little things children do should be done calmly and quickly. For example, it is not worth getting annoyed about a child coming to school with no tie. Yes, the school has a rule and it needs to be upheld, but not at the expense of the learning climate you are cultivating.

How not to deal with it

Here are a number of interventions that are not recommended.

'Where's your tie, Peter?' This is pointless because he will say 'At home'.

Or 'Why aren't you wearing a tie, Peter?' Again, an unnecessary question which keeps the whole class waiting. He will answer with an excuse like 'I couldn't find it.'

Or 'This is the third time this week that you have forgotten your tie. What's the matter with you, Peter?' This simply highlights your own lack of consistency because you have let him get away with it up until now.

Or 'Right, that's it. Go to the Head and tell her why you have forgotten your tie. I don't have time for this, I'm busy and she made the rule anyway!' Oh dear, this is very unprofessional as it reveals a crack between the teacher and the Head that children may want to try to widen. It also shows a weakness. The teacher feels that she cannot deal with it and has to use the 'big guns' for such a trivial thing.

How to deal with it

'Hi Peter, are you okay? . . . (usual civility) . . . I see you haven't got a tie on today, (acknowledgement). I will speak to you about it later . . . take your seat.'

This shows you have logged the broken rule and asking whether he is okay allows him to tell you if anything serious has happened that may explain why he has not got the correct uniform. Children whose parents are separated may spend the weekends away from home and this can disrupt their usual routine. Getting uniforms right may be one of the difficulties of such arrangements. Drawing attention to the tie shows the whole class that you have noticed it and speaking to him later indicates that he has not got away with it. In a quiet time you can use a pre-planned response such as:

'Peter, we have a rule about uniform and ties. Can you tell me it?'

'Ties should be worn at all times in school except during PE.'

'That's right, Peter. I want you to go to the office and ask to borrow a tie for today and then to ensure you have one tomorrow, okay?'

'Yes Miss.'

'All right, have a nice break and I will see you later.'

Notice how the teacher finishes the meeting with a common courtesy. This rebuilds the relationship and demonstrates to the child that it is not a serious issue.

Careful consideration and planning will pay off. You will feel prepared and confident. You will also have settled on your own style for remaining calm and can begin to refine it.

■ Using humour

It is amazing how a sense of fun can make most things move along more easily. Everybody likes a person who is able to laugh and who can smile at things when they go wrong. Children, especially, like a teacher who can inject some fun and humour into the lessons. That does not mean that you should become flippant or irresponsible, simply be able to use a little humour in the right places.

When things begin to go wrong and the heat starts to rise, the situation can quickly be defused with a few well-placed comments. When you find yourself getting wound up or overly defensive, humour can prevent you getting in deeper. Where sarcastic comments exacerbate a situation by forcing the recipient to become defensive, humour can provide a useful outlet.

The ability to be funny is not a gift particular to only some people. It can be learned and confidence can be improved by imagining you are an actor. It does not have to be the real you. Assume you are a comedian and your attitude will change. Try it out when a child attempts to be insulting; it may even get the children on your side.

These examples demonstrate how the heat can be taken out of potentially stressful situations. However, care should be taken when using humour to prevent your replies coming over as put-downs. Children who make these kinds of comments are usually lacking in confidence and looking for attention. Humorous replies allow their inflammatory remarks to be acknowledged but offer a response that they will probably not expect. The attention is moved away from them and the wind is taken out of their sails. This is particularly effective with the more embarrassing incidents that occur in class, such as the following.

A child perks up with a comment like 'Is that your old Fiat Punto in the car park, Sir?'

This could provoke a reply like 'It's not old (which it is actually), now get on with your work!'

Alternatively, you could try the humorous reply: 'Yes, I can do 0–60 miles an hour in five minutes. Not bad, eh?'

Personal comments like 'Sir, that shirt is a revolting colour' may result in 'Don't be so cheeky or I will keep you in at break.'

Using humour: 'I know, I must learn not to mix light and dark colours in the washing machine.'

Case Study

The class have been working on a report about rivers on a recent Geography field trip. They had been working silently for five minutes and doing well when suddenly the silence was broken when one of the boys passed wind loudly so everyone could hear.

Boys can be quite crude at times and events like this are extremely hard to avoid. When they happen they cannot be ignored. They usually prompt a wave of laughter and feigned asphyxiation. There is little chance of it going unnoticed by the rest of the class who will take the opportunity to stop work and engage in humorous and silly behaviour.

Preventing the problem is difficult. It is not easy to raise the issue in a serious discussion and you can hardly have a rule like 'Passing wind is forbidden in lessons.'

How not to deal with this

'Who did that? Stand up immediately!'

This is unlikely to get a response and will lead you into deeper conflict if you pursue it.

Or

'Stand up or I will keep you all in after the lesson until someone owns up.'

A whole-class detention will always cause problems and you will be seen as grossly unfair.

Or

'Whoever made that foul noise/smell must leave the room immediately.'

You will probably not even be heard because the class will be laughing and your irate, serious response will become the target of their ridicule. Either way, you will be on the losing end. You cannot get a child to own up and take you seriously because they will not want to submit to you. You will need to be cleverer than that.

The positive, pro active approach

There are some preventative measures you can try for these kinds of incidents. Teaching social skills like politeness will provide a way in and can be done during PSHE lessons or circle time through discussions about the kind of behaviour that is acceptable in your classroom. Unsociable behaviour may include sudden out-bursts, silly noises, humming, tapping and clicking sounds. The mention of burping and passing wind might provoke a few giggles but you will have made your point.

Older boys will pass wind loudly to gain attention. The reaction from the rest of the class will be about the smell and will be over-exaggerated. Your response should be quite decisive and as unobtrusive as possible.

'Robbie, that was very rude. Pack up your things and go to . . . (your class time-out area or another class as agreed between staff beforehand).'

'But Miss, I couldn't help it.'

'Maybe you couldn't and we will discuss that at the end of the lesson. Now go and I will come and see you when the bell goes.'

The child will have to negotiate his return to the group and agree to observe the behaviour code in future. Do not enter into any discussions or arguments during the lesson. Alternatively, you may feel you do not want to take it this far, so a simple response with a deferred consequence could be used.

'Robbie, that was rude. See me at the end of the lesson.'

Then turn away – do not respond to any reply, just continue with the lesson.

Sometimes you will not be able to tell who the culprit is so your response should be minimal. Open the windows and tell the children who are over-reacting to stop being so silly and continue with their work. The children who cannot be sensible and quieten down will need to be given an activity that demands atten-tion and concentration such as a short period of note-taking. There is nothing like copying down a few notes from the board to get the class back under control.

'Phew! What a stink, etc.'

'I'll open some windows.'

'You pig! That was evil.'

'Right, this seems to be a good time to make some notes of the key points. Take out your pens and copy off the board please.'

Alternatively, you could try humour as an effective means of taking the heat out of the situation. The children who over-react are obviously not really suffocating so you could play along with the gag with phrases like:

'It's windy in here today!'

'Someone over-did the beans at lunchtime!'

'We really must have a word with cook about the dinners!'

'Whoever did that trouser puff is in dire need of some serious dietary advice.'

This will probably defuse the situation, put an end to the play-acting and give rise to general laughter that can then be allowed to die down. You can get the class under control more easily because they will not find your quips as funny as their own show of amateur dramatics. You will still have to deal with the incident if it occurs again but by showing you have a sense of humour you will deter the children from deliberately doing it to wind you up.

Humour is a great vehicle for building relationships and developing a rapport with the class. It shows you are able to have a laugh and that you do not take everything too seriously.

Case Study

Two boys were arguing about a football and who should have the ball. The teacher approached and asked them to give him the ball. Then he said: 'You both seem to want it at the same time so I have an idea that will resolve this. You have got to say your name backwards and whoever makes me laugh the most gets it.'

They each had a go and the teacher decided that they were both very funny so he said: 'Mine is DIVAD THGIRW. Yours were both funny so I am going to bounce the ball between you and you both have to go for it.'

The boys seemed to think that was fair and went away laughing and playing together.

Using controlled anger

There is a distinct difference between being angry and being annoyed. Understanding the difference and being able to demonstrate annoyance while still controlling your anger is a vital skill that all teachers should develop. We are the adults and we must take a lead in modelling the behaviour we want our pupils to learn. Anger is an emotion that takes over our rational responses. It can become so powerful in some people that it takes control to the point where they say they cannot remember what happened. They use phrases like 'I just lost it' to describe what happened.

We will get annoyed about things we see in our classrooms but we should make sure we communicate that annoyance in a clear, unambiguous way, by qualifying exactly what the child or class has done. Comments should be directed at the behaviour, not the child. It is no use getting angry and shouting at the class because you will just be showing the children that you have lost control. So try to avoid the following: 'Right! That's enough. I've had it with you lot! You've made me so angry!'

Definitely steer clear of making irrational threats like: 'You have gone too far this time. You are going to regret this!' And worst of all: 'I am not going to take this anymore. Get out and go to the Head you stupid boy!' (or words to that effect).

All of this achieves nothing and generates a very harmful atmosphere. You will be left with feelings of failure, guilt and helplessness.

You have every right to get annoyed when things pile up and it seems like the whole class are hell bent on messing around. You have a choice, either to express your concern in a calm, assertive way or to show your annoyance. Let's look at how these strategies can be used.

Name-calling

Children will call each other names and they are not always doing it to hurt. It is something many children do when they are with their peers and it has become so habitual that they often do not realise they are doing it. We need to draw the line because name-calling can be very destructive. There are some teachers who are prepared to accept it and excuse its use by describing it as street language. This is a mis-guided view. Street language belongs out on the streets, but in the classroom a different set of standards apply. Name-calling does not belong in a positive learning environment and needs to be addressed in a direct way.

Case Study

The class were engaged in a technology project making gift boxes and bags. A boy at the table near the window called across to another nearby: 'Pass the glue gun Josh, you "Gay Boy".'

The teacher heard this and indicated that she wanted to speak to him. 'Ricky. Could you just come over here please so we can have a quick chat?' She turned and started walking to the door, expecting him to do as she asked. 'Why, what have I done? I haven't done nuffing.'

'Ricky, I just need to have a brief chat with you.' But Ricky decided not to move. In this situation the teacher could not force him to move so she reminded him of the consequences of not doing as he was asked. 'Ricky, if you don't come over for a talk you will have to stay back at break instead.'

This will usually get the pupil to comply. Ricky got up and reluctantly walked across to the door, cussing and tutting. Once the teacher was sure he was coming over to her, she turned to the class to direct them. 'Carry on class. I just need to talk to Ricky.' Then she turned to him and expressed her annoyance as concern in order to remove the personal emotion.

'You called Josh a name just now.'

'I was only joking and he doesn't care. We do it all the time.'

'I care Ricky. I am concerned that you are calling other children in our class names like that. What is our rule about name-calling?'

This refocused Ricky on the rule he had broken and enabled the teacher to use her behaviour code rather than get emotionally involved and possibly end up losing her temper.

Children will say and do all sorts of things that can annoy. I certainly get annoyed and angry at times, especially when a child goes on and on, repeatedly disrupting my lessons or making personal comments like: 'I think this is boring and you get on my XXXXing nerves!'

Obviously, this kind of thing is not terribly common in mainstream primary schools but the response is the same wherever you work: 'I am not speaking to you like that so do not speak to me in that way.'

The response is direct and gives back the choice to the child by helping them think about how it feels to you.

There are occasions when you may need to show you are extremely displeased. This is when you use feigned anger. You remain in control but give a convincing performance so that the children know you have a ferocious side that you keep locked up. Do not over-use it and always switch back to being in control immediately so they only get a glimpse of your anger. If you do have to resort to this, remember:

- direct your anger at the behaviour, not the child;

- use responses beginning with 'I';

- explain what is apparently making you angry;

- redirect at the end of the sentence.

Offering praise and encouragement

Praise is the easiest reward to give and in many ways the most powerful. Positive classrooms are characterised by the use of praise and encouragement. Negative comments and put-downs are sidelined and challenged so that the children will feel safe and secure.

Support and encouragement are vital elements in enabling children to tackle difficult things and take risks with their learning. It inspires confidence and willingness to have a go. However, we need to be guarded in how we give praise if it is to have the effect we want. Children prefer being told they are good or wonderful to being reprimanded but it is unspecific praise so it holds less currency than individual, targeted praise.

Nurturing a positive climate requires the use of praise and encouraging comments in significantly larger proportions than criticism. It is worth trying to offer praise approximately four times more often than criticism. This may seem difficult at first but the knack is in finding good in the little things. Even the most disruptive and naughty children will do some things right so it is more about changing your personal perception. Do not think to yourself that you expect children to do things right as a matter of course. Teach them your routines and ways of behaving, then praise the children when they do something how you want it. This is a powerful means of helping children manage their behaviour. When an individual does something right and you praise them for it, they will feel good and provide the rest of the class with an example to copy.

A child who is not sitting up attentively can be corrected in a negative way:

'Don't slouch like that, Shane.'

Or positively:

'I want you to sit up straight Shane.'

Alternatively the teacher could tactically ignore the pupil and find some children to give specific praise to.

'Amy and Robbie are sitting up straight and ready to go, well done.'

This use of praise works well in a variety of situations.

'Good work Shelley for remembering to put your hand up.'

'Thank you Andrew and Caroline for remembering to sit with your legs crossed.'

The use of directional language combined with praise helps to create a positive atmosphere.

'Don't rub out mistakes like that!'

sounds much better as

'Use the eraser softly to make a clean correction.'

Rephrasing a criticism as a directional phrase and giving it to the pupils who are doing it correctly reinforces what you want rather than what you do not want.

'Can't you use a ruler?'

sounds better as

'Kwame, well done for remembering to use the ruler to underline the title.'

Turn your reminders into positive experiences for the children.

'Don't leave your coats in that mess,'

sounds like you are nagging rather than directing the child.

Changed to

'Emma and Hassan, thank you for remembering to hang your coats on your pegs'

is much more preferable.

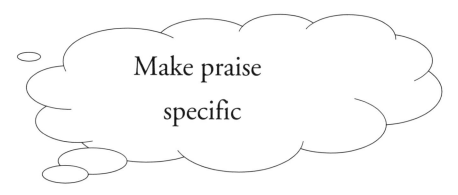

Make praise
specific

As you can see, specific, qualified praise directed at a child rein-forces what they have done right and rewards them for it. This can be applied to verbal feedback about work and also written feedback on work.

'Neil, I can see you have started your sentence with a capital letter, well done.'

'Sarah, your handwriting looks beautiful since you have been concentrating on keeping it on the line.'

'Gemma, I have been watching you take turns and letting others go first. That is very thoughtful of you.'

Encouragement can also be given by helping children to recognise their own achievements. This is done by asking a specific question.

'How do you think you have behaved this lesson, Roddy?'

'How do you think your presentation/talk went, Samantha?'

'What do you think of your effort this time, Megan?'

When they start to give their answer, you can pick up on positive things that they say.

It is very easy to forget things that children have done well because of the hurly-burly of the school day. It can also be difficult at times to give praise. A solution is to have a list of the children and put a tick against their name if you encourage or praise them during the day. Alternatively, put their names on the board when they do something worthy of praise. You will be able to see whether you have missed any children and then you can do something about it before they go home. You do not need to keep the list going, unless of course you find it useful, because you will eventually get used to praising the children frequently.

Modelling good manners

Whatever you do in the class will be observed by the children. When you correct a child, the rest will be looking and when you give instructions, rewards or sanctions, they will be witnesses. They will judge you as much on what you do as on what you say, so it is worth remembering that and making a point of modelling what you say to reinforce it. Saying one thing and doing the opposite will confuse the children and eventually they will copy your actions rather than heed your words.

There are teachers who will lay down very good foundations based upon respect and valuing everyone and then contradict themselves by treating the children as if they were insignificant.

Case Study

Mr Smith had been coaching his Year 6 class about remaining calm when things didn't go their way. He had been working with them on thinking before they reacted to avoid getting angry and ending up shouting and being aggressive.

Paul had been mucking about in Science and eventually he went too far. He knocked a beaker filled with salt solution on the floor and it smashed. Mr Smith went berserk and started shouting. 'I've had enough of this behaviour. You are behaving like a Year 1 kid. All year you have been pushing it and you have never done as you were told.'

The class were stunned. He had always told them that they needed to try to keep calm and certainly never shout.

'Get out of my sight. Go to the Head and tell her what you have been doing!'

The message the teacher was giving was that shouting and losing your temper was all right.

We need to begin by regarding the children as human beings and treating them in the same way that we would wish to be treated. The one thing we all have in common is that we all have feelings and it is important that we show the children we are aware of this through the little things we do. Throughout this book I will be emphasising this. Remembering to say 'hello', 'please', 'thank you' and 'excuse me' is essential in communicating to the children that we are aware of their feelings. We cannot get away from the fact that children do develop their own moral code based on how they are treated so we must give them good role models and set good examples.

Goal disclosure

It is fitting to close this chapter about language and communication with an explanation of a linguistic technique for dealing with poor behaviour. Rudolf Dreikurs *et al* (1982) developed this technique for getting to the reasons behind certain behaviour exhibited by an individual. The process is called 'goal disclosure' and can be used to help children think about the reasons behind their actions. It is best carried out in a quiet place away from the noise and activity of school life at a time when there will not be any external demands or interruptions. The process involves:

- adopting a neutral, friendly manner;

- sitting at right angles to the pupil;

- being relaxed and relaxing the pupil before you begin;
- using structured questions with a reminder, an inquiry, then an illustrative explanation;
- finishing with an agreement.

Here is an example of a typical 'goal disclosure' session.

Case Study

The reminder

Johnny had been acting as the class clown.

'Johnny, you know you sometimes make funny remarks in lessons?'

The inquiry

'Do you know why you do it?'

Pause and wait for a response. The child's most likely reaction will be to either look down or aside. They will not usually make eye contact with you.

The next part of the interview is extremely important. You need to handle it sensitively in order to help the child to get the feeling that you understand why they did what they did. This is done by suggesting the most likely reason without giving them a feeling of insecurity.

The illustrative explanation

'I would like to tell you what I think was the reason. Is it that you want people to notice you and like you? When you make the other children laugh, does that make you feel good? Do you get a buzz when you know you have entertained us?'

The child may either answer these questions or make some movement or sign in his expression that indicates that you are on the right track. Dreikers calls this 'recognition reflex'.

The agreement

'I realised that you were trying to make us laugh by cracking the jokes, making clever comments and the funny noises.'

When the child denies it and says that was not the reason, you answer with 'Oh, I thought that was what you were trying to do. Can you say why you like to make the comments, jokes and noises?'

This allows the child to give his own reasons. Then you can try to understand them and start to work with the child.

The disclaimer

Make sure you let the child know what you can and can't do so he will realise you are not going to change the interview from one of support into an interrogation. It is not a case of 'Ah ha! I thought so and now I am going to make it really difficult for you or punish you.' This will only trigger a negative response and engender distrust. First state the limits: 'I can't force you to stop making the comments and funny noises in lessons.'

The partnership

Show the child what you want and how they can be involved in finding the solution.

'What I really want is your help to find a way to control your interruptions.'

Then work with the child on devising a plan that will give him some control over his behaviour. In return, reward him with praise, encouragement, your personal time or whatever will work for him.

The plan should begin with an audit that the child does during a lesson to find out how often he presents the behaviour that needs addressing. The audit can be used to discuss targets and strategies to use in future lessons.

■ Summary

This chapter has been about the way we talk to children. The underlying tenet is about treating the children as human beings who share the same feelings as you. Therefore, it is worth considering how you would like to be treated and start modelling it so they can learn from you.

▨ Review

Your voice is a powerful tool. Use it carefully.

Always insist on silence before you speak.

Give clear, simple instructions. Do not move on until everyone understands them.

Try to say 'yes' rather than 'no' when children want something.

Do not react emotionally. Take time to think.

Use humour to defuse a difficult situation.

There is a place for controlled anger but only show it sparingly.

Praise children. They will respond well when their efforts are recognised.

Make praise specific.

Model good manners.

Chapter 5

Avoiding conflict

The day-to-day business of teaching is a potential minefield of conflicts and therefore it is vital to develop ways of avoiding it for your own sanity. Calm and peaceful learning environments do not naturally occur in primary schools. It stands to reason – you have thirty children cooped up in a room together for five hours every day; given the choice, most of them would rather be out and about, no matter how much fun you may make your lessons. However, schooling is compulsory and so we must make the best of it. I have seen many teachers opt for the easy route and expect good behaviour, only to find themselves fire-fighting incident after incident because they have not planned in advance. Forward thinking can convert a conflict situation into an opportunity for you to reinforce your behaviour code and remind the children of your rules, while providing positive feedback at the same time.

So this chapter is essential reading in your quest for classroom karma. It will help you:

- focus on the behaviour, not the child;
- set clear boundaries;
- develop a hierarchy of responses;
- learn to tactically ignore undesirable behaviour;
- use redirection constructively;
- practise the 'look';
- use positioning instead of words;
- consider the power of body language;
- ask questions and change the subject to defuse incidents;

- understand primary and secondary behaviour;

- give directions with choices;

- use choices with conditions;

- see the value of taking a child aside for a private word.

From minor to major

All too often teachers make a mountain out of a molehill when dealing with pupils who misbehave. Why do they do it? It is exhausting, disrupts the atmosphere and interrupts the flow of the lesson. Furthermore, any capacity to deal with more serious incidents will be gone if it has been used up on the small stuff. The skill is in matching your intervention to the incident so that it is in proportion to the misdemeanour. A lot of the disruptions that occur in the classroom can be dealt with quickly and unobtrusively so that the lesson can continue. Over-servicing minor incidents will lead to conflicts that could have been avoided.

Focus on the behaviour, not the child

This is the golden rule. Labelling children as naughty, bad, difficult and even horrible, nasty and downright awful can have long-lasting effects. Calling them 'slow', 'thick' and 'stupid' will turn them into victims. They will think that they cannot change because they have been judged and that's it. The rest is obvious. They will give up and become what you have called them.

This can be avoided by focusing on their behaviour. Show them that you like them but dislike the behaviour they have chosen. Help them to see they have a choice about the things they do and the way they act. They can always change their behaviour, but they cannot change who they are.

Children will have their moments of thoughtlessness when they make poor choices or fail to follow your instructions, but do not take it personally. Always remember they are making a bad choice, they are not bad children. This will enable you to manage the behaviour rather than control the child. Control involves the removal of choice. Without choice there is no responsibility. The aim is to teach children to take responsibility for their behaviour.

■ Develop a hierarchy of responses

Good behaviour management systems have varying levels of response that will allow staff to deal with a wide range of incidents that occur in schools. The first level is in the classroom and is dealt with by the class teacher. They will handle the less serious incidents. When they have exhausted their strategies or the child is not responding to the strategies, a referral on to the next level will need to be made. A teacher will immediately refer a serious incident, such as a violent assault or abuse, without going through the first stage.

The second level will be managed by someone with a year group or key stage responsibility. Alternatively, it could be the SENCO. They will have had experience dealing with more complicated incidents and may want to call in the parents and other agencies to find a solution.

The final level is the senior leadership team. This is usually the Deputy or the Head Teacher. When the referral reaches this level it is extremely serious. The kinds of incident that get through all the other stages are:

■ hitting a teacher;

■ racial or sexual abuse;

■ bullying;

■ leaving the school without permission;

■ actual harm to another pupil;

■ possession of knives or other weapons;

■ drugs or alcohol;

■ malicious damage to school or personal property.

As you can see, these are all very serious. The reason for having the various levels is to keep incidents in proportion and deal with them using consequences that are appropriate. Staff get into difficulty when they refer minor incidents straight to the top. I have been in many schools where it is common practice to send a child to the Head Teacher for frequent low-level disruptions such as talking in lessons. The reason teachers do this is because they have either run out of strategies or they have not been applying their own consequences effectively. Alternatively, it is because they have had enough and want to get the child out of their room. Whatever the reason, it demonstrates that they are not coping and the school needs a proper system. It is a waste of the Head Teacher's time dealing with small incidents that should be handled by the teacher. So where do you start?

Set clear boundaries

Children want boundaries, they like the security that they provide. When boundaries become blurred or disappear, children get confused and problems occur. It starts with small incidents and niggling low-level disruptions, which become more frequent and increase in scale if they are unchecked. When this happens at home, all kinds of difficulties arise. Parents who cannot set or enforce rules find themselves being dragged into a power struggle. Their children challenge and win. They realise they have won but they cannot cope with the freedom. For example, the parents may not be able to keep them in at night. The result is a child roaming the streets until they decide they want to go home. They come into contact with older children and hang out together. They do things in an effort to be accepted by the older children and end up acting in a manner that is way beyond their years of experience. Groups of unsupervised children out on the streets will eventually do silly things in an effort to amuse themselves and before they know it they are on the wrong side of the law. You can spot these children if you look carefully. They have a swagger and an attitude that seems to exude confidence. They are eight-year-olds acting fifteen. They will show little apparent interest in things their own age group would like because they have to keep up an act. The burden of behaving much older puts a lot of pressure on the child.

Boundaries are one of the most important things you can give children. They will respect you for showing them what they can and cannot do. When they make a challenge you need to stand firm, be resolute about what you want and follow through with consequences to teach the children what is unacceptable.

Do not fall into the trap of assuming your pupils know what the boundaries are. Teach them the rules and what the consequences will be if they break them (see Chapters 6 and 8). You will have your own expectations for behaviour so make sure you explain them to every child in the class. You will also have your own expectations for work. These may include how it is set out, when it is due in and neatness. You will probably want to tell them how they should work when they are in groups, how much freedom they will be allowed and what group presentations should be like. The key to success is in the communication. If you make sure everyone knows the rules and what is expected, you will have already gone a long way to reduce conflict.

Learn to tactically ignore undesirable behaviour

Tactically ignoring is a conscious choice that we can make to selectively ignore a specific incident. We are fully aware of it but decide that it is better to ignore it than stop the flow of the lesson in order to respond. This strategy is ideal for coaching young children by shifting attention to those who are doing things right.

Case Study

The whole class was discussing what they would do if they were faced with a dilemma. The teacher asked a question and most of the children who knew the answer put up their hand. One or two called out: 'Sir, Sir . . . I know,' etc.

It is not a major issue but it can lead to problems. It certainly doesn't merit a consequence – that would be far too draconian. After all, the children are trying to participate in the lesson and enthusiasm should not be punished. They just need some help in how they go about it. This is done by ignoring the children calling out and choosing a child who has their hand up and is waiting silently to see whether they will be asked. Reinforce the direction when you select the child.

'Katy, you have your hand up, can you tell me?'

or

'Thank you for putting your hand up . . .'

This approach will help most attention-seeking children to follow your directions, but be wary of the child who is used to getting his own way because he will persist.

'Answer me! Stop ignoring me or I'll start shouting louder!'

Obviously a response is required when this happens. Not only is the child ignoring your direction but they are also being very challenging. Give a calm, assertive reply such as:

'When you put your hand up I will let you answer.'

or

'I will speak to you about your interruption at the end of the lesson. In the meantime, if you put up your hand and wait I will let you answer.'

This redirects the child and shows you have noted the challenge but chosen to defer dealing with it so the lesson can continue.

Tactically ignoring can be used for dealing with children who are being silly and acting in an inappropriate way.

Case Study

Robby and Jordy were sitting together and pushing each other in a playful way. Mrs Green could see what they were doing as she scanned the room but did not want to draw attention to them. She knew they liked to be the class clowns and enjoyed having an audience. She finished what she was doing, paused, then said: 'Okay, let's see which table can be first to sit up straight, arms folded and eyes on me . . . GO!'

The whole class jumped into action and within seconds were as still as statues. 'Well done, Green Tribe, that was very quick. Blue Tribe all have their eyes on me.'

She praised each table as they did what she asked. Robby and Jordy quickly forgot their messing about and followed suit. Children like to do the same as the rest and they usually want to please. Mrs Green made a mental note to reorganise the seating plan to split up Robby and Jordy to prevent them getting into any more trouble.

Sometimes a child will go into a tantrum when they do not get their way. Ignoring them can be a powerful means of getting them to stop but it can also be quite time consuming and wearing.

Case Study

Danny was working with several other children in a small group with Tina, the learning support assistant. The Reception class had been working on their numbers to ten in Numeracy and had been pretending they were shopping. Danny wanted to be the person who did the till but he had already had his turn and one of the other children was next. He decided to collect up some of the plastic fruits they were using and took them over to the window ledge and sat on them. Then he started tapping the window with a banana and shouting:

'I want to do the till.'
'I want to do the till.'
'I want to do the till!'

He went on and on and on for some minutes. Tina did not rise to the bait. She went to the cupboard and got some more of the fruits. Then she said to the rest of the group: 'Okay, a new delivery of fresh fruit has just arrived. Jayne, you do the till. Rebecca and George can be the customers. Line up now and be ready to ask for what you want.'

'I want to do the till.'
'I want to do the till.'

'Those are nice-looking apples, Rebecca. Why don't you ask for three apples?'

'I want to do the till.'

'Rebecca, count out loud as you put them in Jayne's bag . . . one, two, three. That's right, Rebecca.'

Tina did not let Danny get the attention he wanted even though he was making so much fuss. She went on with the game and eventually Danny realised he wasn't getting anywhere. After a little more protesting he stopped and just sat quietly. Then he picked up the fruit, went over to the shop and joined the back of the queue. Tina acknowledged him and after a minute praised him for waiting quietly in the line. It had worked. She had ignored him until he did what the others were doing and then she praised him and brought him back into the lesson by talking about the fruit he was going to buy.

Children who do something wrong and are challenged may some-times show their displeasure in an attempt to shift the attention from themselves. They will do things that are designed to wind you up and eventually you will be worn down by their behaviour.

Case Study

Tom was in Year 6 and looking forward to leaving primary school. He had really had enough of all the things they did. He had started to get cheeky and a number of other boys had joined him. They challenged the teachers regularly – not in a serious way but they did not just take things when they were told off. On one occasion Tom and his friend Steve were told to step out of the dinner line and wait because they were messing about. Then Mr Pearce, the teacher on duty, came over and spoke to them. Tom stood with his hands in his pockets and an arrogant expression on his face. He clearly had a very challenging attitude and felt that he should not be told off because he was in Year 6. Mr Pearce noted his attitude and could have been side-tracked and made a comment about him having his hands in his pockets or his defiant expression. He chose to ignore it and concentrated on what Tom and Steve had done wrong.

'We have a rule in the dinner hall and that is to line up in single file in your class groups.'

Tom was pouting and looking away as if he didn't care.

'You were jumping the queue and pushing the Year 4 girls.'

Steve tried to protest and Tom was staring at Mr Pearce in a disdainful way.

'You can rejoin the queue at the back or go away and come back at the end.'

'That's not fair,' protested Steve.

'You're always getting at us,' said Tom.

Mr Pearce resisted these invitations to get involved, repeated his instructions and pointed to the door. They both turned around and started to walk out. Tom swaggered past the queue in an heroic way, muttering to himself: 'It's lousy anyway. The dinners are crap!' Mr Pearce knew better than to respond and tactically ignored their attempts to get the last word.

The skill is in knowing when to ignore a child's behaviour. Often it is straight after you have given a direction in order to give the child time to think and eventually choose the right behaviour, e.g.

> *'Richard, we have a rule about talking when we are getting ready to go to dinner. It is to sit in silence with your arms folded.'*

Then tactically ignore the child and reinforce your direction by going to pupils who are doing what you have asked. Encouragement and affirmation should always follow once the child carries out the direction.

> *'Well done, Richard, I can see you are sitting quietly. You can join the line now.'*

It can be difficult to remain calm and ignore all the rude behaviour, so it is well worth rehearsing what you will say when those situations arise.

Case Study

Billy got out of his seat as the lesson came near to the end. The teacher spotted it and corrected him in a clear, assertive way.

> 'Billy, you haven't been given permission to leave your seat so go back and sit down please.'

Billy had a little tantrum and eventually returned to his place, huffing and tutting. Once he was sitting, he folded his arms in a very expressive way and sighed loudly several times. The other children noticed it and so he acted up even more for their benefit. The teacher ignored him and scanned the room looking for children who were doing what she had asked.

> 'Sasha and Keiron are sitting properly, that's an extra house point for both of you.'

This prompted the rest of the class to check out Sasha and Keiron, then fold their arms and sit to attention in an effort to earn house points as well. Billy followed suit but if he hadn't done so the teacher would have begun the plenary by issuing a challenge:

> 'I want everyone who can remember something a plant needs to grow to put up their hands when I say "Now", not before.'

Children like Billy will probably find the challenge irresistible. He tried to get attention on his terms but failed. The teacher switched her attention to the children who were behaving well. Then she moved on with her lesson, leaving Billy struggling to attract an audience that had become far more interested in what she was offering. Eventually he gave up and joined in and the teacher recognised his compliance with a few words of praise and an opportunity for him to contribute.

▪ **Use redirection in a constructive way**

Watch children when they have been caught in the act doing something wrong. Some children will become experts in diverting the blame away from themselves by providing intricate excuses and far-fetched stories. It is easy to get drawn aside from what you were originally trying to do, which was correct the child. There are some kinds of 'bait' that are guaranteed to get you going if you do not guard against them. Personal comments about the way you look, dress and act are typical. Some children will even make rude gestures and call you names.

Case Study

Simon was deliberately avoiding work. He had already made up excuses about why he couldn't get on. Mrs Watts, his teacher, had tried on a number of occasions during the lesson to get him on-task, to no avail. After several failed attempts Simon could sense that the teacher was beginning to get frustrated because he was not doing as she wanted and he started to get cheeky.

> 'I am not going to do this work, so don't stare at me like some kind of poodle.'

Mrs Watts felt he had gone one step too far and she took umbrage.

> 'Don't talk to me like that!'

'Like what?' replied Simon in a confrontational way. He had a faint smile on his face. 'At least I don't have a stupid accent like you!'

'How dare you . . .'

The teacher was in too deep and had got involved. She failed to pick Simon up in an effective way when he was rude. She invested emotional capital in the intervention and came out the weaker.

Case Study

Amanda was chatting to her friend and the teacher spotted her. When he told her to get on with her work and talk later at break, she got defensive.

'Hazel started it by asking for a pen.'

'No I didn't. I already had a pen. You asked me if I had heard the new single by XXXX.'

'You cow! I did nothing of the sort.'

'Sir, did you hear what she called me?'

'Stop it you two. Swearing and calling each other names is not allowed.'

'Yes but . . .'

'I said stop it or you will have to go to the Head.'

'But what about HER?'

The teacher should have redirected after Amanda accused Hazel. If he had intervened and issued a warning for her to be silent and put up her hand when she wanted something, the rest could have been avoided.

Redirection is the first step in getting a child back on track before you have to resort to warnings and consequences. It may not happen immediately, so you should always allow some take-up time. If the child still does not do as you ask you can either give a warning or repeat the direction. I use the 'broken record' method (Smith, P. and Thompson, P. 1991) of repeating a direction quite often. It can be highly effective when you use an assertive voice and an authoritative expression.

A response to any remarks a child makes when they are trying to divert attention from themselves is to partially agree with them.

'Tony, keep the noise down, thanks.'

'I was talking about the work, Miss.'

'Maybe you were but you should be working in silence.'

Rogers (1994) describes this as 'dignifying'. It can be hard when the comment is aimed at you personally.

'Your breath smells!'

Your natural response is to react to the comment. However, you need to remain in control and focus the child back to their primary behaviour by redirecting them.

'Yes, I won the Manchester Men's Extra Hot Curry Eating Championship last night. Now would you like some help getting started?'

The teacher partially agrees using humour and brings the child back on-task with an offer of help. Let's look at another example of this with a Year 5 pupil.

'Scott, I can see you haven't started work yet. Would you like some help?'

'No!'

'So you know what you need to do?'

He mumbles to himself but does not start the work.

'Okay Scott, you have ten minutes left to get it finished', (refocus).

'It's boring. We did this yesterday.'

'Maybe you did but this is the work we are doing', (partially agreeing and redirecting).

No further response is needed. You walk away and give the child some time to think but expecting him to begin. When he does, return to him and check he is all right, offer help and give praise. If he does not get on with the work, you cannot make him, so refrain from making comments like:

'You still haven't started! You are wasting time. You WILL do the work or else I will make you do it at lunchtime!'

This will push the child into a corner. He has no way out without losing face. He is trapped and will probably get frightened. He will react in one of two ways. He may break down in tears or he may come out fighting. It is better to remind him of the inevitable consequence and leave him to make the decision.

'I can see you haven't started work yet (a statement of fact). I offered you help but you said you didn't need it. I am going to give you a warning. If you choose not to do the work now I will keep you back at lunchtime.'

Nine times out of ten the child will get on with the work, but if they do not they will be making the choice and the consequence will be inevitable. At least with this way you will have avoided a confrontation.

▓ Practise the 'look'

What is it about some teachers that children find different? They will tell you that certain teachers are 'really strict' or 'not to be messed with'. Yet when you watch them in action, there is no sign of aggression or overly draconian methods. It is not until something more serious happens, or when a child repeatedly misbehaves, that you suddenly become aware of what the children mean. The teacher is able to make an expression that is so powerful that the children are frozen. It is a look that they are able to use with great effect. Children know it and know when to fall silent and behave. The teacher's expression is one of 'I can't believe what you are doing and I will not tolerate this behaviour!' No words are necessary.

The 'look' says it all and saves a lot of time and energy. It is probably one of your greatest assets, so it is well worth practising. Watch other teachers around the school. Those who have mastered it will be able to command instant respect. The children will not want to risk crossing the teacher. The look says 'Mess with me at your peril!'

The assembly had begun and the children were sitting listening to the teacher who was telling a story. One boy leaned over and whispered something to his friend. The teacher paused for a moment, just long enough for the boy to realise that something was amiss. He looked up to see the teacher staring straight at him. He became locked into eye contact with her. A feeling of paralysis came over him. The other children knew she had spotted someone misbehaving – they knew that look. Some surreptitiously glanced sideways to see who she had in her sights. They were careful not to make it too obvious – they didn't want to be given the same treatment.

The teacher made no comment, just stared at the boy in that same way some teachers do, long enough to make him feel uncomfortable. He bowed his head in a kind of submission, ashamed he had interrupted her assembly. Then the teacher slowly turned back, smiled at everyone to put them at their ease and resumed her story.

All that without having to say a word! The trick is to imagine you are an actor. You know your 'look' is an act but you make it as realistic as possible. You are using it to get what you want. You expect the children to recognise and respond. They are deferring to you as the adult in charge.

Use positioning instead of words

Proximity can have a powerful effect. Picture the school hall during public examinations. Do you remember how it felt? You would be working away on your GCSE or A-level examination paper and the invigilator would be walking around slowly, up and down the aisle. You were aware of their movements and footsteps, then they would stop somewhere just behind you. Silence. There was a feeling of someone nearby watching you. Even if you were not doing anything you still felt uncomfortable. This can be a useful strategy when a pupil is off-task. Combine positioning with 'the look' and you will not need words.

Case Study

Paul had strayed from the task set and was looking out of the window at the other Year 4 class doing PE in the playground. He had spotted one of his friends and was signalling something to him. Ms McCready had looked up from the group she was helping a moment before he started gesticulating and guessed he was up to no good. She concluded her discussion with the group, stood up and started to walk round the room towards Paul's desk.

When she reached him, she stood slightly behind him and made him aware of her presence but avoided looking at him. About half a minute elapsed, then Paul realised she was standing right near him. He turned away from the window to face the front again. Then he glanced sideways to see what she was doing. She appeared to be staring intently at some children across the room in the corner. He picked up his pen, pulled the book towards him and started work. The teacher waited for a few minutes, then, once she was satisfied that he was working went to help another group. There was no need for her to say anything. Her proximity had made him feel uncomfortable enough to get back on-task. If need be, she would have given him one of her 'looks' but it was not required.

■ Body language

We can communicate so much through the way we act. Visual cues can be much more powerful than the words we are saying and it is worth considering how these signals can be used to your advantage. To illustrate the point, if you stand at the front of the room, legs slightly apart, hands on hips staring at the class expectantly, the children will stop what they are doing and shift their attention to you. The signals you will be giving are associated with authority, assertiveness and power. Someone in charge who is going to get what they want and the army sergeant major is an extreme case of this.

The opposite of this is hunched shoulders, stooped posture and fleeting glances around the room without engaging in direct eye contact. The message that these actions convey is of someone who is uncertain, anxious and possibly even frightened.

Turning this knowledge to advantage needs some forethought. There may be rare occasions when you want to appear as a sergeant major, but usually just more assertive. This is achieved by leaning against the teacher's desk, half sitting and half standing. Place your hands at your side on the desk and look straight at the children in a relaxed, open, easy style. Shift your attention to groups who are not responding quickly enough until every child has fallen silent and is looking straight at you. This should not be rushed. If you do not wait for every child to do it you will have shown that their individual attention is not required.

There are a number of unobtrusive hand signals that can be used to convey specific messages. These include:

Good, well done   Be quiet   Stop!

Calm down   That's good

There are other signals such as a wink for 'well done', 'I'm with you on that one' and 'I agree'. These signals will enable you to quickly communicate with individual pupils without having to say a word. They are useful for dealing with minor disturbances. The knack is in matching your body language with what you are saying to create the maximum impact.

Try to avoid certain actions because they could lead to conflict instead of avoiding it. A finger being wagged in a pupil's face while you are redirecting them will antagonise. Moving too close so that you are invading a child's personal space will certainly make them feel uncomfortable. If a child is under stress, angry or feeling frightened, close proximity could result in them lashing out at you, so stand back. Clenching your fist or shaking a fist at a child will have a negative effect as well. The best approach to use when a child is upset and angry is to remain calm and appear unthreatening. Approach them with open hands held at your side. Do not put your hands in your pocket because they may think that you are going to pull out a weapon. When dealing with a very disturbed child, approach them with an outstretched arm and an open hand facing them. This will protect you from things being thrown at you or spitting but will still give the child the signal that you are not a threat.

Height is an obvious means of showing who is in charge. Standing near small children will require them to look up. Get the taller ones to sit down when you need to redirect or reprimand them, to accentuate your height. The reverse is necessary if you do not want to appear threatening. You may want to give a child some help so it is best to get down to their height to reduce the effect. I will often kneel or even sit on a chair near them so I am at their eye level.

■ Ask questions

When a potential conflict is imminent, questions can be used to help defuse the situation by distracting the child. Ask one of the children involved a question about the lesson to shift their attention away from the argument and back to you. Outside of lessons, questions about their interests and hobbies will have the same effect.

Case Study

Aidan and David had been playing a game of tag in the playground and they had collided badly. Aidan picked himself up and was aware of the other children looking on, which made him feel embarrassed. To save face, he looked for David who was also just getting up nearby. He launched into a stream of verbal abuse, blaming David for not looking where he was going. David automatically retaliated and started cussing at Aidan, saying he must be blind.

I had seen the collision and was on my way over to see whether they were hurt when I heard Aidan's outburst. I called him, as I got nearer. 'Aidan are you all right?'

'Yeah but that idiot wasn't looking and went straight into me.'

Turning to David I asked: 'David, did you have your radar switched on?'

He looked quizzically at me. Aidan was standing nearby, still fuming, so I turned to him and inquired: 'Aidan, how do those space ships in *Star Wars* get around without crashing into things? They seem to go so fast. They must have a special gizmo on board to help them.'

Aidan and David forgot their disagreement and began describing the ships' automatic guidance to me. After a minute or two I told them I had to go and left them talking animatedly about space ships. A potential fight had been avoided by turning the incident into a shared interest.

This method works well in all kinds of situations. Pupils who have strayed off the task can be pulled back with a question like: 'How's it going, Lucy?'

The girl will probably turn around and open up her book and reply: 'I was just starting . . . but I didn't have a pencil.'

An intervention is unnecessary because she will know she has been rumbled. You may decide that a warning is required to make the point that time wasting is a poor choice. Perhaps a comment like: 'The work needs to be finished this lesson and if it is not you will be staying in at break to complete it.'

Walk away at this point and assume that the child will get started. Do not stand over them as if to say 'Come on then, I'm waiting' because that would be like waving a red rag to a bull. The child may need a little time to process your direction but in most cases they will decide to get on with the work eventually.

Questions will provide the child with an ideal opening to make excuses that will detract from their behaviour. Try to avoid asking questions:

'What are you doing?'

'Why did you do that?'

'What's going on here?'

The lesson was Art and the class was Year 3. Two boys were flicking water at each other with their brushes. The teacher shouted across the room at them. 'What's going on over there?'

Actually it was obvious. They were having a great time playing with water, something most children enjoy. They were certainly not cleaning their pallets, which is what they were supposed to be doing.

'He flicked water at me Miss,' said Zafer accusingly.

'He started it by spraying the tap on my pallet,' protested Adam.

The teacher was now faced with a difficult situation because she had not seen the whole thing so she could not make a fair judgement. She should have asked a directional question that forced the boys to refocus on their behaviour and what they had been doing.

'You are taking a long time. What are you supposed to be doing?'

'Cleaning our pallets, Miss.'

'Then finish and go back to your seats, quickly now.'

You may find that a child will answer your question with 'I dunno!' or 'Nothing Miss'.

If they do, redirect them with an instruction: 'You should be cleaning your pallets and then return to your seats ready to leave.'

The clear direction foils the deliberate attempt to torpedo your question, leaving the child with limited options, either to do the right thing or to face the consequences.

■ Changing the subject

This is a favourite strategy of many parents with babies and tiny tots. Watch when a toddler falls over. The parent will whisk them up, whirl them around and make a funny face or noise for them. They may suggest that they go in the garden and play or pick up a favourite teddy and move it around in an animated way. Of course, this strategy should be used only if the child is not breaking any rules because it provides an opportunity to alter the behaviour before it becomes unacceptable.

Case Study

The children were working together in groups during the PE lesson, practising their batting and bowling skills. The heat was beginning to rise because one girl wanted to be the bowler but it was not her turn. The teacher acted quickly to defuse the situation. She asked one of the other children to bowl and moved the girl behind the stumps to keep wicket. She talked to her about the importance of being able to catch the ball and get the person batting out by touching the stumps.

Case Study

The children were on the carpet during their Literacy lesson, listening to the teacher reading a story. She paused and then she called the children out to read a few sentences each. Danny was fidgeting and trying to get the attention of the boy sitting next to him. The teacher ignored him at first but then realised he was not going to stop so she intervened. She called out his name and then asked him to come out and turn the pages of the book for her. He sprang up and went to the front with enthusiasm. He had read the book as well so that he could turn the pages at the right time. This refocused him and removed him from the situation where he was beginning to lose control and misbehave.

The move to include all children in mainstream education may be resulting in more challenging children being in schools. Perhaps you have one of these children in your class already? Some children may have witnessed domestic violence or even been the victims of physical or sexual abuse which has damaged them psychologically. Such children can become violent at times so distraction is a very effective means of managing them.

Case Study

Wasim was a wilful child with a history of being abused sexually and physically. Eventually he was taken into care and fostered. He could be really nice at times but more often than not he would be aggressive when he was asked to do something he did not want to do. Psychiatrists suggested that it was not the activity that was the problem. He would suddenly get very anxious during the day. There was no warning, it just happened. Their explanation was that he was worried that his foster parents would disappear like all the other adults in his life who were supposed to care for him. He would do anything to get home to check that they were still there, even try to be excluded. He felt he needed to stay at home to prevent them from going. He had been told that if he behaved well he could eventually go back to live with his parents but he dreaded this so he misbehaved to ensure he stayed with his foster carers.

The staff developed a range of strategies that included the use of distraction to try to break the cycle of misbehaving. When Wasim began kicking off they took him aside and started a game of football or catch with him. They also got him talking about something they knew he found interesting such as Arsenal football team or motorbikes. The effect was almost instantaneous and within minutes he was calming down. The other remarkable thing was that he would agree to do what he had refused to do earlier. The 'red mist' had passed and the staff were spared the physical confrontation.

■ Understanding the primary and secondary behaviour

Children will exhibit two kinds of behaviour when things start to go wrong. The first is called the primary behaviour and is associated directly with the incident. For example:

- ■ fighting
- ■ off-task activity
- ■ talking over the teacher
- ■ flicking pellets
- ■ playing with the water tap

These are just a few of the examples and you should refocus the child when you intervene and challenge them.

Secondary behaviour is the distraction. It is the smoke screen a child uses to hide their primary behaviour. They use it to deflect the blame from themselves to another person. For example, a pupil who repeatedly kicks the chair of a child in front may be told to stop by the teacher and replies with comments like 'I'm bored!' or 'Why are you always picking on me?' or 'Don't shout at me!' These comments will shift the emphasis from themselves to the teacher, so it is important to resist the temptation of getting involved. The most effective response is to refocus the attention back on the incident by saying: 'I am giving you a warning to stop kicking the chair and get on with your work.' Then record the warning on the behaviour log (see Photocopiable materials). 'If you continue you will be choosing the consequence which will be to sit at the time-out table for the rest of the lesson.'

The redirection, followed by the warning of what the consequence will be, allows the child to choose for himself what he will do.

▨ Give directions with choices

Directions are a neutral means of getting children to do things. They differ from orders and commands in that they are not demands. They feel different from the receiving end because of the way they are delivered. They form part of a cooperative relationship whereby the child recognises they are being helped and accepts the direction. It is a transactional relationship based upon the status of the teacher as someone who is enabling the child to learn rather than forcing them. Pupils who fail to follow directions are choosing. The alternative is when the relationship is based on control. The person has submitted to the authority. For example, soldiers and prisoners are forced to follow orders. Refusing to follow orders can result in serious consequences such as court marshalling or being discredited, struck off or even physically punished.

Giving directions in a clipped, abrupt way will make the children feel they are being ordered around. Adding simple courtesies like 'please' and 'thank you' changes the tone, e.g.

'Take your cap off in class!'

can be changed from a command to a request by adding 'please' so the child knows that it is something you want that they can do.

'Chris, will you take your cap off please?'

A direction like this could cause problems because the child may refuse and then you have to deal with that. The solution is to make the direction a transactional one by building in a choice. This empowers the child by giving them an alternative course of action.

'Chris, can you put the cap in your tray or on my desk please?'

Notice how the direction has been changed with the addition of the child's name, two choices and the use of 'please'. The child will consider the choices and opt for the one they prefer. In the case of personal possessions, they usually choose a space they have control over such as their tray, bag, drawer or coat peg. More serious incidents can still be dealt with in this way but the choice is between doing what you ask or a consequence.

'Gemma, turn around and get on with your work or you will get a warning.'

The warnings lead to consequences and Gemma is empowered to decide for herself. If she makes a poor choice that leads to a consequence, she will have been the one in control of her behaviour and cannot claim she is a victim when it happens.

Be specific

Name the child before giving the direction so they know who you are addressing. This will ensure they are alert and attending to what you are about to say.

'Donna . . . (pause for attention) . . . can you show me your left hand please?'

This identifies Donna as the only person to answer and the children will get used to waiting rather than putting up their hands and calling out.

There will be times when the commands are necessary to ensure safety and prevent accidents or serious incidents. These should be given in a firm, clear way.

'Stop!'

'Move away from there!'

Return to a quieter voice once the instruction is given.

Using choices with conditions

These can be very effective and you will often hear parents saying, 'If you do this, then you can do that.' Some may describe it as a form of bribery but Rogers (1994) calls it a conditional choice. The child makes a request that is granted once they have completed what you want. Then they can have what they asked for.

Case Study

Martin was trying to speak to the teacher but she was ignoring him because he was calling out instead of putting up his hand. He persisted.

'Mrs Collins, can I tell you what I did last night?'

In the end she turned round and replied: 'Go back to your seat and put up your hand, then you can tell me.'

She gave a direction and only when Martin did what she asked was he allowed to talk.

Case Study

It was break time but the class were not calm and ready for work.

'When you are all sitting silently, I will let you go out to play.'

Again, the teacher gives a conditional choice. If they want to go out they have to do as the teacher asks first. If not, they wait inside and miss out.

Sometimes a child will behave in an unacceptable way and you can either tactically ignore or use a conditional choice to help them focus on what you want. This is particularly effective if the child is repeatedly disruptive or avoiding getting down to work.

Tom had not applied himself. He had spent most of the lesson daydreaming. The teacher was aware of his time wasting and had offered help but Tom had declined it. She allowed him a short period of time to get going and when he didn't she warned him that he would have to do the work at break. At the end of the morning she dismissed the rest of the class and kept Tom back. Then she gave him a conditional choice.

'You chose not to work in the lesson and stay in at break and do it instead. The rest of the class has gone out to play and when you have done your work you can join them.'

Tom knew that if he sat and wasted time he might not get out before the end of break so he got on with it.

Children will continue mucking around if they are not challenged, but if they are given a conditional choice they are more likely to make a good decision. Later, at a convenient time, you should rebuild the relationship and discuss the incident, showing the child how the good choice they made led to a personal reward for them. In Tom's case he got some of his break outside with his friends.

Conditional choices can take the heat out of a situation. The emotional impact of a command is replaced by an instructional tone necessary to describe the choices available. The attention the child has to give in order to make a decision can prevent a confrontation.

Case Study

Year 6 were lining up for dinner and collecting their trays. Christian and Connor were larking about, pushing in and annoying the other children. Mrs Samson, the midday assistant, noticed and went over to them.

'Stop it, you two, or I will get Mr Jones (the Deputy on dinner duty).'

They ignored her and kissed their teeth under their breath. She was annoyed by that and responded.

'Don't be so rude. I am sick of you lot! Just because you are in Year 6, you think you can do what you want. Now get in line or I will report you!'

They laughed at her and pushed into the line near the front. The other children complained because they were jumping the queue. Within minutes they were all protesting.

What Mrs Samson should have done at the start was to offer a conditional choice.

'Christian and Connor, I have been watching you trying to push in. Go out of the dinner hall and either join the line behind Sabrina or go away and come back when all the Year 6 have gone in.'

If they had objected and stayed in the line, she could have instructed the cook not to serve them until they did what they had been asked to do. In that way she would retain her authority and show them that she has the power to decide what happens rather than having to get the help of a teacher.

This approach works well for parents at home.

'When you have done your homework/music practice/chores/tidied your room, you can have the PlayStation/watch TV/use the phone/go out to play.'

▧ The value of taking the child aside

There will be times when it is better to take the child aside or out of the room to talk to them about their behaviour instead of doing it in front of the whole class. The benefits will differ depending upon the incident, the child and the context. In some cases it will enable you to handle the incident more efficiently. Children like a show, especially if the teacher is getting emotionally involved. They will become distracted and the child misbehaving may be looking for attention. Removing the child from the audience will resolve both of these difficulties and enable you to deal with the incident with more authority. The child will not be able to gain confidence from knowing they have an audience and so will be less inclined to challenge you.

There are some children who react very badly if they feel others are watching. Stepping outside and being discreet could make the difference and avoid a negative reaction, which is out of proportion to the incident. It will also be possible to deal with it in a calm way once you are away from the public arena. You can also try to find out why the child is misbehaving. They may have a legitimate reason. Some understanding will often resolve situations. So try to listen to the child's point of view and weigh it up before acting.

Personal accounts are usually required when there has been an incident involving two or more children. In these cases you should separate the individuals and isolate them by sending one to a different classroom where they can write their account. They will not be able to confer and cook up a story and so you will get more of the truth. Children usually end up incriminating each other and the truth comes out more easily once they attempt to pass the blame.

■ Summary

This chapter has been about avoiding conflict using a wide range of strategies, but there is no substitute for the most important one of staying calm. The tendency will be to get emotionally involved as your physical reactions prepare you. Try to recognise the signs. Your heartbeat increases, your breathing gets faster and nervousness sets in. The more serious the incident, the more pronounced these changes will be, but do not let your emotional side take over. Stay calm, collect your thoughts, lower your voice and make a mental note to speak slowly. The effect will be powerful. Children will expect you to get angry and when they see the opposite they will be thrown and start to soften.

Managing behaviour in a positive way is not a gift. It is one of the tools of the trade and you will need to learn to do it through practice. Now you have read this chapter, take some time to decide when and how you will develop these skills. Maybe you might like to ask a colleague to help by observing and feeding back to you.

◼ Review

Focus on the behaviour not the child.

Use a staged response from low to high intervention.

Tactically ignore undesirable behaviour.

Standing near a child can get them back on-task.

Remind children of the direction when you intervene.

Use 'the look' when you do not want to break the flow of your lesson.

Distract a child when they kick off by changing the subject.

Using hand signals can be an unobtrusive way of correcting or acknowledging good behaviour.

Sometimes it is best to take the child aside and remove the audience.

Offer choices with or without conditions.

Do not respond to secondary behaviour.

Chapter 6

Values, beliefs and expectations

We live in a society where people have become more confident in challenging authority and the hierarchies. They are far more inclined to assert their rights now than children were forty years ago in my school days. How often have you heard the phrase 'I know my rights'? This is good in many ways. The centuries of exploitation of the masses by a small majority of privileged, often wealthy people who led charmed lives resulted in a fixed organisation of society that went unquestioned. It is only when people recognise that something is unjust that a challenge can be made.

With rights comes the responsibility to uphold and protect them to ensure that everyone shares the benefits. That is why limiters are in place. They may be rules enforceable by the state; they may be mutual agreements such as the codes of conduct adhered to by commercial companies which advertise on television; they may be collective understandings that form our moral and ethical codes. Examples of this include queuing, turn taking or not calling someone a racist name.

Schools are microcosms that share many of the same values as society at large. All schools have rules and teachers attempt to articulate and enforce them in their classrooms. This is done with varying degrees of success that often depends upon the style and method the teacher employs. Problems with behaviour in the classroom usually occur because the teacher has failed to communicate their expectations for behaviour to the pupils. They make an assumption that the children know how to behave and will adhere to the rules. However, children come to school with very different sets of experiences and backgrounds. They may share many of the same values but be unaware of how to express them in the classroom setting. This is where the work needs to be done to bridge the gap by teaching the children about their rights and also their responsibilities as part of the group sharing those rights. The pathways from values to the desired behaviour is shown in Figure 6.1.

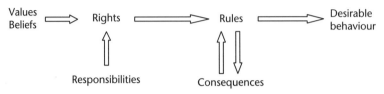

Figure 6.1 Pathways from values to the desired behaviour

The way to ensure children become aware of your expectations and their roles is to teach special lessons at the start when you first take over the class. Going through the process with your class will result in the development of a code of behaviour that they will feel ownership of. It will contain the underlying values that form the foundations for the rules, directions, rewards and consequences.

▪ The objectives of the behaviour code

The behaviour code will help you establish a positive atmosphere in the classroom so you are free to teach and your pupils can learn. It will focus your thoughts on how you deal with a variety of incidents and enable you to plan your responses rather than have to struggle when things get difficult.

Case Study

Lorna was having a really bad day. The night before she had been working on her plans for the next half term and researching resources on the Internet. It had been very productive but she had become so engrossed in what she had been doing that she lost track of time. It was gone midnight when she finally got to bed.

She awoke next morning with a splitting headache. It was fatal working on the computer late into the evening. She always slept badly and she knew she would pay for it. Her headache would not go away despite taking a long hot shower, drinking herbal tea and trying to stay calm and breathe deeply. Things just seemed to get worse and she felt she really could not face her class that morning.

When the children arrived the problems began. Callum had brought in a toy even though he had been told not to on numerous occasions. One of the other boys took it and an argument broke out. Lorna managed to sort them out and then got on with the register. Numerous other minor incidents and distractions occurred throughout the morning and by break she felt she really wasn't coping very well. The final straw came when Julia accused her friend Sue of taking her pen with the fluffy top.

Lorna blew at that point. She could not contain her temper and shouted at them to stop and sit down. Then she scolded the whole class for their constant poor behaviour and inability to settle. She knew later that this was quite unfair because it wasn't 'constant' and also only a few of the class were actually involved. At the time she did not know what to do and simply reacted.

'I've had enough of this. You can all stay in for break to pay for your poor behaviour. Perhaps then you will be better behaved.'

She was really suffering and should have gone to the staffroom to relax and get her energy levels up ready for the next lesson. Her irrational response resulted in the pupils feeling she was being unfair and she was losing her own time because she had kept the class in.

The behaviour code is a blueprint for the children to learn how to take responsibility for their behaviour. It is not a set of orders. It is a framework of rules with related rewards and consequences. The children are free to make their own choices. The teacher's role is to show them how good choices lead to positive outcomes and poor choices lead to negative consequences.

Martha was a big character in every sense of the word. She towered above her Year 4 group and she had an ample figure with her imposing bosom and broad beam. She was a jolly person and cruised around the classroom clucking and chuckling as she went. But make no mistake, she was no pushover. If any child so much as put one toe over the line of what was acceptable, they were for the high jump. She kept a firm hold on everything and was described as very strict. When she gave an order, every child jumped to it. They were safe in her hands. They didn't need to think about how to behave, she told them. There were no problems with discipline in her room.

That was why she got very cross whenever another teacher took her class. There were always incidents. One supply teacher even described them as the worst class she had ever taught. She couldn't believe how rude and lacking in motivation they were. She had organised the children into talk partners. They were supposed to discuss the main characters in a story they were planning and then list the qualities under headings of appearance, family, favourite pastimes, hobbies, etc. Well, they didn't even get going. They chatted, some got up and walked around and several even started doing other things.

Martha blamed the cover teacher – she thought she was obviously weak and couldn't manage the class. They were not a difficult group so she must have been too soft and given them too much freedom.

In reality the children suddenly found themselves leaderless. The supply teacher was expecting them to work in a more independent way than they had been used to. Without clear directions and tasks that involved doing exactly what they were told, they were at sea. They were being given freedom that they could not cope with and ended up trying to take control of what was going on because the new teacher did not seem to be leading them in the tight way Martha used. Without rules, rewards and consequences, there was just chaos. The new teacher did not know how to check them and so they went unchallenged.

One fundamental purpose of the code is to ensure the safety of everyone in the room. This safety goes beyond being protected from the risks of fire and dangerous activities. It is to protect children from bullying and intimidation, name-calling and fighting. The rules should clearly state the expectations otherwise children could become perpetrators and victims of these forms of behaviour.

Case Study

Kirstie looked back on her first year of teaching with mixed views on how it had gone. The one thing that really disappointed her was that she did not know much about managing behaviour. She had not prepared a behaviour plan and had no systems in place in the classroom to help the children with their behaviour. She somehow imagined that they would behave for her. She thought she would have to tell off a few children every so often but that was all.

The first few weeks went all right and she did not really notice any problems. Then one of the boys came to her complaining that the others had been calling him names at break. At the time she dismissed it as the usual playtime behaviour, not worthy of any special attention. But it persisted and then she noticed it happening in the lessons as well. The other thing that came to her attention was the low-level banter including some swearing. She tackled each incident and told the children it was unacceptable but that didn't seem to have much effect. Just before half term, she got a complaint from a parent who told her that her son had been losing pens, pencils and other small personal things. Kirstie asked why he hadn't reported the loss but he would not give a satisfactory answer.

'Well, I can't really do anything if I do not know about the incidents,' she explained.

Half term passed and then the parent returned and informed her that her son had revealed that the things had actually been taken by another boy in the class. He said that the boy had forced him to give the things and told him that if he told he would regret it.

'It would seem you have a bully in your class and I want to know what you are going to do about it,' she said.

To top matters, an able boy who had complained that he was being called nasty names reported that a little group who sat near him kept saying he smelt. They refused to sit in any chair he sat in or touch anything he had touched without making a big deal of wiping it.

All Kirstie could do was go and tell them off, threaten to send them to the Head and plead with them to stop what they were doing because it was not nice. Things came to a head at Christmas because a number of parents came to see the Head about the incidents in Kirstie's class. It seemed that there were two groups of boys and one group of girls making the lives of the others quite intolerable.

Luckily the Head was understanding and recognised the problem that had caused the incidents and then helped Kirstie to set up a behaviour code to prevent things happening again. She needed some rules to establish what was unacceptable and she needed some consequences to deal with the problems when they occurred.

Learning is a complex process involving a range of experiences that the learner needs to review and evaluate to ensure that it has become secure. Learning takes place most effectively in a safe, secure environment. The code helps us to develop a positive climate that will enable all children to learn and progress. They cannot learn if they feel insecure or threatened. They will not want to venture out of their comfort zone and take risks.

Case Study

Molly was a great believer in the idea that you need to make mistakes in order to learn. By analysing errors for yourself or with the help of someone else you can work out where you went wrong and avoid that pitfall next time. She had observed other more experienced teachers using these methods and had been impressed with how the children had engaged with the idea.

She tried to develop the same climate in her own lessons and always approached any child who had made an error with sensitivity. What she couldn't understand at first was why some children seemed to take real pleasure in the mistakes of one or two pupils. It got worse as the weeks passed until eventually she realised that there was a culture of 'taking the Mickey' any time anyone made a mistake or did something wrong.

Molly found out much later that a number of children who were not targets for this treatment started copying answers or writing them in when they were checking them as a whole class. She was horrified when she looked back at the whole sorry mess. She knew what she wanted to achieve with her class but she had failed to pick up the one crucial ingredient that the teachers she had observed had used. They had established the rules to ensure everyone in the class felt secure before they encouraged them to start taking risks.

■ How do you go about drawing up a behaviour code?

You will need to design and deliver a series of special lessons that will enable your pupils to contribute to the code. Have discussions and make sure that everyone in the class is involved. The process begins by finding out what values and beliefs you share as a learning community.

Values and beliefs

We all have our own values and beliefs and we share many of them. They may differ slightly from one person to the next depending on their background, but many are common to us all. Our values and beliefs are expressions of how we wish to be treated and how we should treat each other. Cultures and communities will have their own common values that are usually connected to the concepts of human worth and human dignity. The variations in these can be illustrated in the following examples.

The Hippocratic oath held by medical doctors outlines their duty to save lives and ease suffering. Therefore, they may not assist a patient in the process of voluntary euthanasia. However, the oath could be interpreted differently. Some doctors believe that their role should be to help terminally ill patients avoid unnecessary suffering. Some may even feel that if someone chooses to end their own life they should be legally allowed to help them.

We abhor acts that fall outside of our value system, for example cannibalism, marriage between a brother and sister, abuse of children and the killing of innocent people by terrorists. These beliefs and taboos become deeply entrenched and help us to stay within the culturally acceptable boundaries.

Teaching about values and beliefs

The following lessons are examples of how you can go about this with your class.

Activity

Objective: To enable children to understand and explain their own values.

Resources: Prompt sheets 1–4, whiteboard and pens

Activity 1

Discuss how the children know whether something is right or wrong. Use the prompt sheets to aid the discussion. Write the children's ideas up on the board.

Prompt sheet 1   Right and wrong in the home

What are the right things to do?

- I make Mummy a cup of tea
- I go to bed on time
- I do my violin practice

What things are not allowed because you think they are wrong?

- Taking money out of my mum's purse without asking
- Using the Internet to look at rude things
- Swearing

Prompt sheet 2   Right and wrong in public

What are the right things to do?

- Do not talk to strangers

- Lock up my bike with a chain when I go to the shops
- Pick up things for people when they drop them
- Cross the road at a zebra crossing
- Hold the door for someone
- Call an ambulance for someone

What things are not allowed because you think they are wrong?

- Taking stuff from shops without paying
- Dropping litter
- Shouting or swearing
- Vandalising things and graffiti
- Letting my dog do a 'poo' and not clearing it up
- Hurting or killing people

Prompt sheet 3   Right and wrong in school

What are the right things to do?

- Wear my uniform
- Remember my lunch box/PE kit
- Talk in a friendly voice
- Be kind to the younger children
- Put my hand up when I want something

What things are not allowed because you think they are wrong?

- Talking in lessons
- Playing with toys in lesson time
- Swearing
- Calling other children names and bullying
- Fighting

Keywords: Right, wrong, value, belief, moral, ethical

Activity 2

Discuss the lists and then ask the children to say how they know whether they have done something right or wrong.

Prompt sheet 4   **How do we know whether we are right or wrong?**

If it's right:

- The teacher ticks it
- We get rewarded with a sticker
- An adult may say 'Well done'
- You just know. Don't you?
- I feel happy

If it's wrong:

- The teacher puts an X by it
- You get told off
- You get punished, like grounded or something
- You get a sick feeling in your tummy
- I just do
- The police come round my house

Conclusion: So we all seem to have a clear idea about what is right and wrong and also we can tell when we do something right or wrong. This shows we have clear values and beliefs about things.

Rights

Rights are the basic fundamental expectations we have as humans. They are expressions of our values. They stem from what we value and describe the way we wish to be treated. For example, 'I have the right to walk down the street unmolested.' Rights can be removed from an individual who violates the rights of others. That is why criminals go to prison. They lose the right to freedom for the duration of the sentence because they infringed the rights of someone and broke one of the laws of the state.

Rights are in operation in schools. They enable teachers to get on with their job of teaching. Classroom rights originate from our basic human rights and work in the same way, e.g. a pupil who repeatedly disrupts, obstructs their own right to learn and the right of others to learn as well. They also take away your right to teach.

 ## Case Study

Justine believed children should behave and when Gary kept on disrupting the lesson with low-level chatter, seat rocking, fiddling and turning round, she felt she had no choice but to send him out of the room to stand in the corridor. Once he was out, Justine was able to teach the class properly – but at what price? Gary was clearly not benefiting. What was he learning about the subject or, indeed, how to behave? His exclusion from the class was a punishment and a dodgy one at that. Out in the corridor he was unsupervised. He did not feel very good about himself and could not find a way back from his problem.

Justine's attitude is fairly typical of a lot of teachers. One pupil was spoiling it for everyone so she felt she had to send him from the class, which is a serious sanction. In her defence, Justine felt she had no choice and that was probably true. She did not have a behaviour code with a staged response. It looked like all she could do was to keep telling Gary off. Then when that didn't work all she could think of doing was to send the child out of the room.

A child who infringes the right of the other children to learn may have to be excluded from the class but only after all the other sanctions have been exhausted.

Teaching about rights

Activity

Objective: To identify and list the rights in operation in a school.

Resources: Prompt sheet 5, whiteboard and pens

The big picture: Last lesson we began looking at our values and beliefs. This lesson we will look at our rights so that we can begin to develop rules to protect those rights.

Introduction: Rights are the basic expectations we have as human beings. They are expressions of our values and describe how we want to be treated. Rogers (1994) describes our basic rights as:

- *Treatment right.* This is the right to be treated fairly and equally regardless of religious, cultural, ethnic, sexual or physical difference.

- *Safety right.* The right to feel free from bullying and intimidation.

- *Movement right.* The right to move around the school in a reasonable way.

- *Right to learn.* The right to learn without distraction or interference in a reasonable working environment and with adult help when needed.

- *Communication right.* A right to share ideas, ask questions and express opinions.

- *A right to justice.* The right to a fair hearing when things go wrong.

Activity 1

Discuss the rights of individuals in society. Talk through and find examples in the school for each right. Show suggestions children give as a mind map. Prompt sheet 5 is an example.

Prompt sheet 5

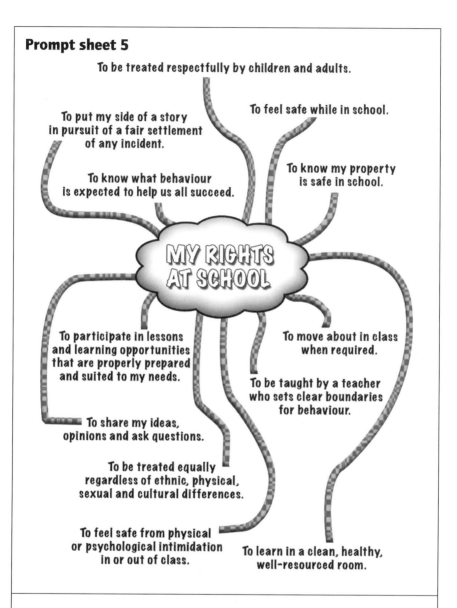

To be treated respectfully by children and adults.

To put my side of a story in pursuit of a fair settlement of any incident.

To feel safe while in school.

To know what behaviour is expected to help us all succeed.

To know my property is safe in school.

MY RIGHTS AT SCHOOL

To participate in lessons and learning opportunities that are properly prepared and suited to my needs.

To move about in class when required.

To be taught by a teacher who sets clear boundaries for behaviour.

To share my ideas, opinions and ask questions.

To be treated equally regardless of ethnic, physical, sexual and cultural differences.

To feel safe from physical or psychological intimidation in or out of class.

To learn in a clean, healthy, well-resourced room.

Activity 2

In pairs, talk about one of the rights and try to identify the role of the teacher and the pupils in protecting it. What do they have to do to uphold it? After about three minutes, share the ideas with the whole class. These are the responsibilities of the group.

Keywords: Right, responsibility, uphold, support, protect, safe, secure, laws, opportunities, individual, community, opinions, boundaries, freedom, fair

Rules

Rules are used to limit excessive behaviour by describing how people should act. They stem from our basic human rights but are more specific to include the differences of a particular community or group. To be effective, rules need to form the basis of all behaviour in the school and be in operation at all times. Rules need to be accepted and owned by the class if they are going to be adhered to, so the children should be involved in shaping them in some way. The rules also need to be simply stated so that everyone understands them.

Teaching about rules

Activity

Objective: To draw up rules linked to rights.

Resources: Prompt sheet 5 (see earlier)

The big picture: We have been looking at how our values and beliefs lead to rights and responsibilities. This lesson we will discuss how those rights are protected by rules. Next lesson we will consider what should happen if any of the rules are broken.

Activity 1

Look at the rights the class thought of in the last lesson and discuss as a whole group what the rule should be for each one. For example:

'To feel that I am safe while in school.'

This right suggests a rule of 'Keep your hands and feet to yourself (no fighting or hitting)'.

The table below is an example of the completed activity.

Right	Rule
To feel that I am safe while in school	Keep hands and feet to yourself (no fighting)
To feel that my property is secure in school	Respect other people's property
To know what behaviour is expected to help us all to succeed	Follow directions given by adults
To participate in lessons and learning opportunities that are properly prepared and suited to my needs	Follow directions
To put my side of a story in pursuit of a fair settlement in any incident	To tell the truth at all times
To move about in the classroom when required	Follow directions
To be taught by a teacher who sets clear boundaries for behaviour	Follow directions
To have my say, share my ideas, express myself and ask questions	Treat others fairly, kindly and politely (no name-calling or swearing)
To be treated equally regardless of ethnic, physical, sexual and cultural differences	Treat others fairly, kindly and politely (no name-calling or swearing)
To learn in a clean, healthy, well-resourced room	Put litter in the bin Respect other people's things including school resources
To feel safe at school, free from physical or psychological intimidation in or out of class	Treat others fairly, kindly and politely (no name-calling or bullying) Keep hands and feet to yourself (no fighting or hitting) Use a friendly voice (no swearing)
To be treated respectfully	Treat others fairly, kindly and politely (no name-calling or bullying)

As you can see, some of the rights share the same rule. You should now be able to develop a set of rules that will work for your pupils. Remember, they need to be framed positively, so avoid the use of 'No' and 'Don't'.

Activity 2

Work either in small groups or as a whole class in deciding which rules you are going to adopt and how they shall be worded. Some sample rules taken from the list above are included below:

Rule 1: Keep hands and feet to yourself (no hitting or fighting).

Rule 2: Use a friendly voice (no swearing).

Rule 3: Tell the truth at all times (no lying or deceit).

Rule 4: Treat others fairly, kindly and politely (no name-calling or bullying).

Rule 5: Respect the property of others, including the school (no stealing or vandalism).

Rule 6: Put litter in the bins.

Rule 7: Follow directions given by adults.

Your rules can be written up and circulated to parents and colleagues. A copy can go on the classroom wall and children should paste a copy in the front of their home–school diary.

Keywords: Rules, rights, home, school, safe, secure, respect, code, conduct, directions

Can rules be enforced?

Yes, they can if they are clear, fair, consistently applied and owned by everyone. The problem arises when the rule becomes difficult to enforce at all times. If this happens, you will need to re-visit it with the children to find out why. For example, a teacher had a rule that stated:

Stay in your seat

What happens when a child needs to wash their brush, get a book, leave the room etc.? The rule could be re-worded:

Stay in your seat unless given permission to . . .

However, this is unnecessary. It is far better to have the rule of:

Follow directions given by an adult

Then you can give more specific directions for specific activities. The other rules apply during the activities but the directions may vary according to what is being done.

What directions will I need?

Start by thinking about the lessons and what the children will be asked to do. List the rules specific to each activity, e.g. assemblies. You will want the children to enter the hall in silence, single file and sit in their class place. They should not chat during the assembly and should leave the hall at the end in single file and silently.

Here are some of the activities you may want to consider:

- group work
- hot seating
- talk partners
- envoying
- whole-class discussions
- practical workshop sessions
- hymn practice
- tests

Think about every aspect of the activity and draw up directions for each one. Imagine yourself doing the activity and try to identify when and where poor behaviour could occur. Keep the directions simple so they are easy to understand. Limit them to no more than four or five per activity. Here are some examples.

Lining up outside the room.

1. Stand still in single file.

2. Face the front.

3. Talk quietly or no talking.

Entering the room.

1. Wait outside in line until you are told to enter.

2. Hang up your coats, put lunch boxes away.

3. Go straight to your place and take out books, pens, etc.

4. Sit with arms folded.

5. No talking.

Registration.

1. Sit in seats facing the front.

2. No talking.

3. Answer 'Good morning/afternoon' or 'Present' when your name is called.

Teaching an up-front whole-class lesson.

1. Put everything away except pen and paper.

2. Look at me. Silence.

3. Raise your hand and wait till I give you permission if you wish to speak.

4. Listen while I am speaking/another pupil is speaking to me.

Working in groups.

1. Stay in your seat; raise your hand if you need something.

2. Do not shout, talk quietly to each other.

3. When I give the signal to stop work, puts pens on the desk and face the front.

Art, Science, Technology activity.

1. Stay at your place; raise your hand if you need something.

2. Only one person at a sink, power tool, etc.

3. Clean and put away all the equipment, tools, paints you used.

Class test or examination.

1. Enter the examination room in silence. Do not talk until the teacher gives you permission.

2. Leave bags and coats outside/at the front of the room.

3. Sit facing the front, eyes on your own paper.

4. If you need something raise your hand and wait in silence until a teacher comes to you.

5. Leave in silence.

Walking in corridors.

1. Walk quietly, no running.

2. Single file, keeping to the left or right (as appropriate to your school).

3. Do not touch displays on the walls.

Assemblies.

1. Enter the hall in single file in silence and sit in class seats.

2. No talking during assembly.

3. Leave the hall in single file. No talking.

Changing for PE or swimming.

1. Enter the changing room quietly. Put all clothes in your PE bag, socks in shoes placed under the bench.

2. Line up quietly at the door in single file/pairs.

After PE or swimming.

1. Line up outside the changing room in single file/pairs.

2. Enter quietly and go to your place.

3. Only (. . .) pupils in the showers at once.

4. Get dried, changed and line up before the bell.

Computer work.

1. Stay in your seat.

2. Raise your hand when you need something. Do not call out.

3. Close programs, return to the desk-top and log off.*

* Schools will obviously have their own specific user instructions.

The directions listed here will ensure pupils behave appropriately. Include these directions in your behaviour plan.

▇ Summary

You are now well on your way to developing a comprehensive behaviour plan to help you achieve a positive learning community in your classroom. The next step is to look at how the rules will be upheld. In the following chapter we will look at the positive consequences as limiters for the rules.

■ Review

- The code is a blueprint for how the children will take responsibility for their own behaviour.

- The code ensures the safety of everyone.

- The code will enable you to develop a learning environment free from teasing and bullying.

- We share many values and beliefs.

- Rights are expressions of our values.

- We are all responsible for upholding these rights.

- Rules limit excessive behaviour and protect our rights.

- Rules are in operation at all times.

- Directions vary depending on the activity.

Chapter 7
Incentives and rewards

■ Introduction

What is it that makes the majority of us law-abiding citizens? Many of the laws seem to limit our freedom and cost us a substantial amount of money. Why do we bother getting road tax for our cars, buying a television licence and paying council tax? The answer, of course, is that we would be fined or maybe even have to go to prison if we did not do these things. We do not want that sort of trouble so we pay and get on with our lives. There is rarely any reward for abiding by such laws. If you buy your road tax you do not get any other benefits. The law is the law and is there to protect the rights of the population either directly by making acts such as murder or theft illegal or indirectly by raising revenue to ensure we have access to the services the government provides. That is the reward.

Changing the way people do things is quite a different story. Behaviour is personal and we all have our own ways of doing things that can be acceptable as long as we stay within the law. For example, the paradigm of manners and etiquette includes an extensive range of customs, habits and rules that are particular to both formal and informal situations. In a restaurant setting the protocol may be to use cutlery whereas it is considered quite acceptable to use your hands at a family barbecue.

Learning the rules of behaviour can take quite a considerable time. Very young children who move from the home environment to school face this challenge. There are new and often quite difficult routines to assimilate and comply with and therefore it is not surprising that some children experience problems. It is in these situations that rewards and consequences become useful aids in training children to behave appropriately.

There are teachers who do not believe in giving children rewards when they behave in an acceptable fashion. They expect children to behave and when they do not, they get annoyed. However, they do use sanctions. They will punish children when they do not do as they are told. It is hardly surprising that children with a teacher like this get put off school.

Young children learn through experience and will quickly modify their behaviour if they are given the right kind of encouragement and are motivated with praise and rewards. They learn to associate pleasurable experiences with the behaviour and eventually it becomes internalised and habitual. That is why rewarding children when they do things how you want them done is so productive.

Using rewards as incentives in the classroom can have the following advantages:

- Children of all abilities can gain recognition.

- Attention is shifted from undesirable to desirable behaviour.

- Self-esteem is boosted, leading to a positive atmosphere.

- Children become motivated to strive to improve.

In this chapter we will look at:

- using rewards to help all children gain recognition;

- avoiding rationing of rewards;

- giving rewards to shift attention to desirable behaviour;

- boosting self-esteem;

- celebrating success;

- considering what rewards to give;

- rewards for individual pupils;

- rewards for the whole class.

Children of all abilities can gain recognition

Positive recognition is for everyone and can be a powerful agent for change if it is used wisely and with care. School is not some kind of Roman amphitheatre where the pupils compete to be champions. It is a place of learning where children are nurtured and helped to prepare for a lifetime that will be productive and fulfilling. Therefore we need to get out of the mindset that everything is a competition because all that does is produce winners and losers, with the majority being in the latter group.

Personal challenge should become the norm. Competition has its advantages, but the balance is wrong. There need to be far more opportunities for individual challenge against personal targets and teachers need to make it possible for all children to find their personal success so they can feel good with what they have achieved. This is done by differentiating tasks so children can access the work at their own level of ability. We should reward completed tasks and individual effort. We must get away from the practice of rewarding only those who come 'top'. Acknowledging those who complete the task to a certain standard will enable more opportunities for giving incentives. A child who finds something difficult and struggles to overcome it should be rewarded to ensure effort and determination become valued.

Do not ration rewards only to those that are the neatest, come top or are the most able

This will create division and work against the aim of building a positive climate for learning for all children. Rewards should be given fairly and children need to know how to earn them. Otherwise, it will have the opposite effect and children will become demotivated.

Case Study

Becky was one of those able pupils who quietly got on with her work but didn't seem to come to the attention of the teacher because she never got into trouble. She just got on with things.

There were several boys in the class who misbehaved on a regular basis and took up lots of the teacher's time. There was also one girl called Alicia who had a problem with her hearing and needed a support worker.

Becky tried to do her work well but somehow she never seemed to be able to do as well as Tricia and Robbie and Jessica. They always got the best marks and earned the most house points. Reports about them were always glowing and when there was an assembly they were chosen to do the best readings and were given the most important roles. Then, when it came to appointing the Head Boy and Girl and their Deputies, of course they got the posts.

There was also a special award called the 'Pupil of the Week' (POW), which was presented in assembly and announced in the newsletter to the parents. Becky would have loved to have won that accolade but it seemed to elude her. Robbie, Jessica and Tricia each won it several times in the winter and spring terms. Other pupils got it as well. Alicia got it for 'triumphing over adversity'. Eric and Nathan won it but God knows why because they never seemed to do any work. A couple of the other kids, who were described as having 'special needs', won the award as well. By the summer term, a group of kids who hadn't got it at all renamed the award 'Pet of the Week'. Becky had talked about it with her parents when they asked her why she hadn't won it. She told them she thought the award went to either the kids who came top or the naughty ones or those with special needs.

Becky finally got the award at the end of June but by then she had become cynical about it. She felt she got it because the teacher had realised that there were some kids who hadn't received it.

This is a good example of how rewards can be misused and end up being devalued.

Well-timed rewards can be used to turn a challenging group around, but you should not expect the same level of behaviour from them as you might from a more moderate class. They will probably not be able to behave for the whole lesson. The solution is to provide more opportunities for them to earn recognition and to allow some mistakes.

Case Study

Monica knew she was taking over a difficult class in September. They had a track record of being a hard group ever since Year 2. There were a number of children with special needs for learning and some 'known' characters who were noisy and a bit excitable. Monica was not going to wait and see how they would be and find out that they were too much for her. She discussed the class with a friend who had had several different groups like this one. She suggested a behaviour code with rewards and consequences that were going to be easy to organise. More importantly though, she outlined how she had increased the opportunities for all the children to earn more rewards by dividing the lesson time up into ten-minute blocks. Any child who behaved well and didn't get a warning or consequence earned a point that they banked towards a reward.

Monica tried out this idea and found it was very successful. After a few weeks she increased the time to fifteen-minute blocks and by half term it was up to half-lesson blocks. The children were still motivated to earn points and she also gave them out for things like volunteering ideas and answers in whole-class time, helping others in on-task time and getting packed up quickly.

You may find that the more challenging children are not motivated by the rewards you offer. When this happens you should seek professional advice because they will need their own individual education plan (IEP) with rewards tailored to their specific targets.

How do I use rewards to shift attention to desirable behaviour?

One of the easiest rewards you can give children that they value highly and that costs nothing is your attention. Children want to be noticed. They want opportunities to answer questions or share their ideas in lessons. They like coming up to the front of the class and using the Interactive white-board and some are really desperate to do little jobs for you. You can capitalise on this by ignoring the children who do not follow your direction (see Tactically ignoring in Chapter 5: Avoiding conflict).

> Ask the class to put up their hands and not call out if they think they know the answer to a question. Select only children who follow your direction. The desirable behaviour can be reinforced by saying to the child you have chosen to answer: 'Thank you for putting up your hand and not calling out.' This signals to the children who didn't follow your instruction what they need to do next time.

In the early days of taking over a new class you could also reward any child who follows your direction by giving them extra points. It is amazing to watch the rest of the class suddenly jump to it so they can earn recognition as well.

> Try out these phrases and see what happens:
>
> *'Jane, you have your arms folded and your back beautifully straight. That's an extra point. Well done!'*
>
> *'Salim is facing the front. That's a bonus point for you.'*
>
> Once you have the class trained you do not have to give a reward every time. Miss out sometimes so the children do not know when they will be rewarded.

▇ Boost self-esteem and create a positive atmosphere

Low self-esteem is one of the common factors in children who have behaviour difficulties in school. They may have a poor self-image due to circumstances at home or it may be a product of the school system that favours the children who learn best through linguistic methods traditionally employed by the majority of teachers. The system marginalises children who cannot meet the demands of the curriculum. Those children inevitably feel that they are failures and look for alternative ways of gaining recognition. It may be by being a gang leader, the strongest in the peer group or the most reckless in order that others will notice them. They may seek attention by being the class clown or by bucking the establishment. Alternatively, they may adopt a much more passive, victim type of approach and perceive themselves as simply no good and not able to gain any recognition within the school.

The problem comes with the way teachers deal with children who see themselves in these ways. The child who is trying to get noticed will turn the spotlight on to the teacher when they try to manage the unacceptable behaviour and that simply furthers their aim of seeking attention. They realise they are getting attention and so they continue to do what they are doing.

A positive climate is achieved only if there is the motivation to work for it. It comes from a consistent effort by everyone involved but begins with the adults in the class. The emphasis needs to be on finding good in what children say and do, not in picking out what they do wrong. It is easy to say something is wrong or to correct a child for not doing as they were asked. It is much harder to look for good in what they do, especially if they are excitable or challenging.

The aim should be to praise four times more than you criticise or reprimand. Once you get into the swing and seek out the little things they do well it will become easier. Encourage the children to do the same and reward them for being helpful or supportive towards their peers. Eventually their perception of your role will change. They will see you more as a coach, supporting and encouraging them.

Celebrate success

Make a point of rewarding children publicly. This will help create a culture of achievement and reinforce your classroom behaviour code. There are a number of ways this can be done. Have a board where children and adults can put Post-it notes describing acts of kindness they have witnessed. Encourage everyone to put up at least two notes a week. Use visual charts for recording individual points or stickers and group charts for team points.

Use your classroom assemblies to highlight significant successes and milestones of achievement, both in and out of school. Notify parents of this and ask them to use the home–school diary to let you know of anything their child has done that could be included.

You may have some children in your class who are shy and do not like attention being drawn to them. It is vital that you find out who they are and then look for ways of helping them enjoy their own achievements less publicly. One way of doing this is to help children keep a record of their successes and achievements. By the end of the year the record should show their progress and it also enables you to pinpoint any children who do not have many entries. You can then try to address it.

Publicly giving out rewards can help other children to choose their behaviour.

> *'Melanie, you have earned twenty points so you can have an early lunch pass.'*

> *'Sunraj, you cleared your desk very quietly so you can be first in line.'*

> *'Well done Beverly, you managed to stay in your seat during that activity. You have earned an extra point.'*

So what rewards can I give?

When you stop and think about it, there are so many incentives you can give your pupils. The following list offers some ideas for you to choose from. Select a variety of rewards that range from small to large so that they can be used in different circumstances. Rewards should always be in proportion to the achievement. Points are useful currency for the pupils to use to 'save' towards rewards with greater value.

You will need clear criteria for giving rewards and these need to be incorporated in your behaviour plan. Younger children will prefer different rewards to older ones. Infants will probably enjoy playing with toys during Motivation Time whereas older children will value an early lunch pass.

Rewards can be given to individuals and the whole class. You will need to decide how the whole class can earn rewards and which ones are available to them (see page 155).

Rewards for individual pupils

■ Praise and encouragement.

■ Points and/or stickers that can be saved towards rewards.

■ Certificates.

■ Free time – Motivation Time, Choosing Time, Golden Time.

■ Extra computer time.

■ First in line for leaving at break, lunchtime, home time.

■ First in line for the bus trip out of school.

■ First choice of games in Motivation Time or Computer Time.

■ Seconds at dinner time.

■ Bring in a toy or personal possession to show the class (younger pupils).

■ Sitting next to a friend for one lesson.

■ Monitor or special duty in class, e.g. cleaning the board, feeding the class pet, switching on/off computers, changing the date on the calendar.

■ Captaincy of a table, team or the class.

■ Act as a guide when a special guest comes to the school.

■ Staff the reception desk for thirty minutes.

■ Helping younger pupils with their reading/in the nursery or Early Years Centre.

■ Telephone call home* (see Photocopiable materials for a script).

■ Postcard or a letter home* (see Photocopiable materials for sample postcards and letters).

- A home visit.
- Afternoon tea with the Head.
- Sitting at the top table with the Head at Christmas.
- Vouchers for a local store.
- A special note in the end-of-year report.
- Teacher's special award.
- Trip at the end of term.

The children work towards the rewards by saving their points. You give a point for every noticeable achievement or good behaviour. Once you have selected which rewards you are going to use you should decide on a tariff for each one.

Stickers can be used alongside points. Children like to receive them and there are many companies which produce a wide range of stickers for different purposes. Certificates are also useful and can be given as interim rewards that mark progress. For example, a Bronze certificate when a child has collected 100 points, a Silver certificate for 200 points and a Gold one for when they reach the target.

How can the whole class earn rewards?

Whole-class rewards can be used to encourage collaboration and team-work. The group works towards a common aim and individuals can learn new ways of behaving through peer pressure. These rewards are useful when you have a particular problem in the class that needs addressing with the whole group, not just with individuals. If you are planning to do this, it is worth asking the class what rewards they would like. Do not start with a blank sheet otherwise they will ask for the outrageous. Give a limited choice (see list below) and discuss which ones they would like to work for as a group.

Rewards for the whole class

- House points (as currency).

- Class certificates (to help them make progress).

- Free time.

- No homework days.

- Video at the end of a half term.

- Class picnic or party.

- Trip out of school.

- Head Teacher's Award.

Once the class has agreed which rewards they want to earn you need to set up a time scale. This should be shorter for younger pupils because they need more immediate rewards at first. Then you should decide how the rewards will be earned. Will they be for the whole class or will there be teams within the class? The latter works well if the teams compete against each other to see which one can earn the most points but all the points go into a class pot. When the target is reached everyone in the class gets a reward and the team with the most points wins a trophy. This encourages some competition within the class but does not result in the majority feeling they have worked for nothing.

■ Review

Shift attention from those who do not follow directions to those who do.

Rewards can be helpful at first in getting a new class to adopt your ways.

Rewards should be used liberally to ensure all pupils feel the benefit.

Have rewards for individuals and the whole class.

Celebrate success publicly but be aware of certain children who do not like the attention.

Praise is the easiest reward to give and costs nothing.

Try to praise four times more than you criticise or reprimand.

Use whole-class rewards to try to change a specific problem that more than one pupil has.

Chapter 8
Sanctions and consequences

▦ Introduction

All behaviour has consequences. Rewards are the positive consequences and sanctions are the negative consequences that occur when a wrong choice is made. From here on any reference to consequences will be related to poor behaviour. Using consequences as well as rewards in the classroom can have the following advantages:

■ Children will know that something will happen when they break a rule.

■ A system of warnings will give children an opportunity to turn their behaviour around by making the right choice.

■ You will not need to make things up in the heat of the moment. You will have a procedure with linked consequences.

In this chapter we will look at:

■ what makes a consequence effective;

■ logical consequences;

■ related consequences;

■ deferred consequences;

■ problem sheets;

■ using consequences as choices;

■ 'take-up time';

- do consequences need to be harsh?

- what consequences are available;

- isolation consequences;

- recording consequences;

- how to exit a child from the room;

- what to do when a child will not leave the room.

The purpose of a behaviour code is to help children make choices. It will need both rewards and consequences to be effective. A behaviour code with only consequences will lead to a negative atmosphere. Rewards on their own provide opportunities to motivate but when a child misbehaves, problems will occur.

 Case Study

Tilly was having some difficulty with her class and decided to discuss it with one of her friends. The friend suggested a range of rewards to motivate the children. The idea was a good one and worked fine for several weeks, with all the children enjoying the novelty of earning points towards a list of rewards Tilly was offering. Then Nick, one of the more excitable boys, got carried away and started messing around in the Art lesson. Tilly intervened and warned him to stop but he continued. She was in a quandary because she had not planned for this. She went back to him.

'I have already given you a warning for being off-task and you have chosen to continue so I have no choice but to deduct some of your points.'

'Hey, that's not fair!' protested Nick. 'You said that any points we got were ours because we had earned them and now you are taking them away.'

Tilly was taken aback by his reply and felt he was being rude. She thought he was in the wrong and should not be challenging her in that way. The only sanctions she had were detention and sending someone to the Head.

'You are clearly not following directions and now you are being rude so I am keeping you back at break, so we can discuss the matter further. In the meantime,

I suggest you clear up this mess and get on with your work. If you don't, you will
be choosing to lose your lunch play as well.'

Tilly was half right and was even using the correct phrases. She offered choices,
redirected the child and focused on the broken rule. What she didn't have was a
range of consequences from the least intrusive to the most. Had she used a
system of warnings and small-step sanctions, she might have prevented a small
incident from escalating into a large one.

Teachers who attempt to control will prevent their pupils from
taking responsibility for their actions, resulting in a victim culture. The
child will feel they are not responsible, have no control and are being
made to conform or be punished. The consequences flow naturally from
poor choices when the children are held accountable for their behaviour.
They are not seen as punishments and the result is that the climate in
the classroom changes. The teacher leader assumes a coaching role and
helps the children understand the consequences of their choices.

What makes a consequence effective?

A consequence should have all of the following characteristics if it is to
be effective:

- It should be appropriate. There should be a clear link between the
  action and the consequence, e.g. wasting time in the lesson should
  lead to the pupil making up the work in their own time; dropping
  litter should result in picking up litter at break. Long detentions
  at lunch or after school are not effective and rarely linked to the
  original incidents.

- It should be dislikeable. A consequence does not need to be severe
  for it to be effective, just something children will not want again, e.g.
  staying back at break for one minute will mean all the other children
  have gone and are playing or are in the dinner queue; five minutes at
  a time-out table isolates a child from the group they belong to.

■ It should be the result of choice. The child is made aware that they can either turn their behaviour around or continue and get a consequence. For example, go back to their place or stack chairs at break; choose the black or the blue pen and then get on with the work or complete it later at lunchtime.

Logical consequences

Parents usually teach their children about some of the hazards they will encounter and how to stay safe. Examples of these are:

'If you don't wear a coat you will catch cold.'

'If you put your hand in the flame you will get burnt.'

Children learn that if they do something there will always be a consequence. The strategies described in this book are based upon this assumption.

Consistent application over time will usually result in children making the link between their behaviour and the outcomes (see Figure 8.1). This is why we need to use logical consequences in the classroom whenever we can.

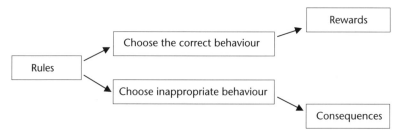

Figure 8.1 The link between behaviour and outcomes

Related consequences

In the past, it was common to give unrelated consequences to the children when they misbehaved. Detention, lines and even corporal punishment were the norm. Corporal punishment was finally abolished in most schools in England in the 1970s but detention and writing lines are still commonly used as consequences.

Effective consequences need to be related to the incident or the behaviour. An integral part of the consequence should be either a discussion or a period of reflection to help the child recognise where they made a poor choice.

Deferred consequence

You can either give the consequence at the time or defer it until later. Immediate consequences could include moving to the time-out table for a short period; coming off the computer if a child is misusing it; leaving the pool if the child is splashing or failing to follow an instruction. Sometimes it is better to defer a consequence to prevent a situation getting worse or interrupting the flow of the lesson.

 Case Study

The class were completing a science investigation and working in small groups. Gary was getting frustrated because things were not going right and decided to have a little tantrum. He pushed some of the papers and pencils off of the desk while in a temper. Carmen stopped talking to a group and went over to see what the problem was. Gary sat with his arms folded, pouting and staring at the floor.

'I can see you are upset, Gary, but we need to get these things picked up. I want you to tidy up the things now or I will have to keep you back at break to do it.'

Carmen gave Gary the choice of putting things right or having a more serious consequence later. Most children will do what is asked of them but some may need some take-up time. Try to avoid lecturing them and focus on the primary aim which is to get the child to clear up so they will learn to respect the room and resources.

Deferring the consequences until later will enable you to discuss the ins and outs of what happened with the child and anyone else involved. The interlude will also give the child the opportunity to calm down and possibly even start to reflect on what they did wrong.

Problem sheet

I am upset because:	Other people involved:	This is what I said:

This is what they said:	This is how it happened:	This is what I will do to fix things:

Problem sheets

The problem sheet (see page 163) can be used in a variety of ways. It is an ideal method for getting written accounts of what happened. It also gives the child something purposeful to do immediately after the incident rather than waiting to be 'dealt with'.

Where more than one child is involved, you should split them up and get each one to write an account. Young children may need an adult to help them complete the sheet. The completion puts the responsibility back on the child. A further addition to this is the 'Interactive Conduct File' (Behaviour UK, www.behaviouruk.com). This is an excellent resource that consists of a piece of software containing video clips of typical behaviour scenarios together with interactive multi-media worksheets. The child watches the appropriate video and then completes the worksheet. It helps them to understand the triggers and the responses by offering a number of options with the related consequences.

Using consequences as choices

A class of children who are really well behaved because they are compliant lack the self-control to behave appropriately when their usual teacher is absent. I cannot emphasise this too often. The basis of a positive climate for learning is in placing the responsibility with the children. This is achieved by ensuring that the consequences are inevitable for the children who make poor choices.

 Case Study

Kerry had been teaching in England since September and had quickly learned different ways of doing things in an English school compared with back home in South Africa. She felt she had got her Year 3 class well trained in how to behave.

It was coming up to break and the class had just packed up. She directed them to line up by the door, one table at a time. Tammy was in line and waiting to be told she could go. Then her best friend, Terri, pulled a silly face that made her laugh. Tammy did a funny little dance with a flamboyant ending. Kerry spotted them messing around and warned them that if they did not wait quietly they would go to the back of the line and wait behind for one minute. Then she turned back to the remaining table of children and began dismissing them. Tammy could not resist the temptation to repeat her little dance because she had enjoyed the response she got from the other children in the line. Kerry was on to her immediately.

'I warned you Tammy, if you couldn't wait in line quietly you would have to go to the back.'

'But Miss, I was just . . .!' she remonstrated.

'You can tell me about it when the others have gone. Now you have chosen to misbehave and be last so I want you to come out of the line and go to the end.' Kerry did not rise to Tammy's pleas. She remained assertive and reminded her of the earlier warning.

This approach shifts the emphasis from you to the children. They know what the consequence of their behaviour will be so they will bring it on themselves if they make a poor choice. Your role is simply to 'broker' the choices.

▧ 'Take-up time'

Children are like adults. They react to situations in different ways. Children need time to consider the options they have before they decide and age can be a factor in their reaction times. In general, younger children will take slightly longer to make up their minds. When children are given directions they need to be allowed some take-up time. Do not be in too much of a hurry. Your patience will pay off.

 Case Study

A child was playing with a small toy he had brought into school, while the teacher was calling the register. He was oblivious to her and didn't hear his name called. The teacher repeated his name and looked up to see why he hadn't answered.

'Adam . . . (she waited until the boy looked at her) . . . put the toy away in your tray or, if you prefer, on my table.'

Adam looked down at his toy. The teacher turned away expecting him to do as she had asked. He sat for a moment or two weighing up the choices and then he went over and put it away in his tray. The teacher finished doing the register then thanked Adam for doing as he had been asked.

You should keep an eye on the child during the take-up time to ensure they eventually follow the directions. If they do not, you will need to return and remind them of their options, which in Adam's case was to put the toy away or get the consequence.

▦ Do consequences need to be harsh?

No, but they need to be fair, consistent and inevitable. So what does this look like in practice?

Fair

The consequence needs to be in proportion to the incident. Giving a severe consequence for a minor misdemeanour is not only unfair but will also create difficulties for you.

Case Study

Carrie was having a bad day. She had been under the weather but had still gone into work because of her sense of loyalty and responsibility. She was not strong at managing her class, not normally a problem because they were fairly well behaved.

It had been raining that morning and the children had stayed in. Carrie had missed her break and was just about hanging on. A couple of the boys were not settling and in the end she sent one of them to the Head because he kept clowning around. It was nothing really. The boys would have settled down eventually if Carrie had had a behaviour code with a series of warnings but she was getting impatient. She just wanted them to be silent.

The problem Carrie has is that she has used the ultimate consequence of sending a child to the Head for a fairly minor incident.

What will she do if one of the children does something very serious? We should always have a clear plan and be prepared for these kinds of days when we are not at our best.

Consistent

Care should be taken to ensure that all children receive the same treatment and if the rules are broken, the consequences should be consistent with previous ones given for the same incidents.

 Case Study

Natalie broke off from explaining how the results of the experiment could be obtained and cast her attention across the room to where the noise came from. Richard was up out of his seat and doing something at the back table.

'The direction was to stay in your seat, Richard. You are up and not doing the work so I am going to give you a warning.' (She noted it on her behaviour log – see Photocopiable materials.) I want you to go to your place and get on with your work. Do you need any help?'

'No, Miss.'

Natalie resumed her discussion with the group she had been talking to. A few minutes later she noticed another boy out of his seat and getting involved with the group on the back table.

'That's enough! Brad get back to your place! I just had to talk to Richard for being out of his place and you go and do the self-same thing! I will not be ignored. You can stay back at break for that!'

'Hey, that's not fair,' protested Brad. 'Richard only got a warning and I am having to stay in for the same thing!' He was clearly frustrated and indignant about the unfairness of it all. Why didn't Richard have to stay in as well?

Natalie had got herself into a difficult situation that was hard to get out of. Brad had a point because Richard did do the same thing. Natalie had dealt with it as if Brad had done it more than once. Brad and possibly others in the class saw her lack of consistency as unfair.

Inevitable

The most powerful consequence is the one the child knows will happen. When you say you are going to do something, you must mean it otherwise the children will treat anything you say next time as merely an idle threat.

Case Study

Sam and Bobby were playing around in the cloakroom at lunchtime, which was against the school rules. They should have been outside in the playground. Meena, a learning support assistant, was on her way to the staffroom and spotted them so she called them over.

'Quick, run for it,' said Bobby and they both legged it out of the other door and across the hall into the other end of the building. Meena called after them.

'I will report this to your teacher and she will deal with you.'

'We're for it now,' said Sam with a worried expression on his face.

'Oh don't worry, she never does anything. She says she'll report you but she forgets. We'll be all right, you see,' reassured Bobby.

A consequence should always happen if you say it will. Whenever something comes up that you cannot deal with at the time, like this example, write a note in your diary for later.

Consequences should be harsh enough to remind the child that they made the wrong choice, but that is all. They are not a means of gaining reparation or revenge. Furthermore, overly harsh consequences can do harm. A child who is given a consequence that is too severe may not learn from it. They may actually turn against you and then things will get much worse.

Long detentions are also a bad idea. They need to be administered and that is usually the job of the person who gives them. Your free time is valuable and will not be used productively if you have to sit through breaks and lunchtimes. The solution is to keep a detention short so that you will always be in a position to do it. As we saw in the example earlier, idle threats lead to a breakdown in the behaviour code.

So what consequences can I use?

Here is a list of consequences that could be useful to you. Choose the ones that will suit your class and school. They are organised into groups: time-trade and related tasks and isolation.

Time-trade and related consequences

- Set out the chairs in the hall for assembly.

- Tidy and stack chairs after assembly.

- Last in line.

- Last for lunch.

- Last in the class when things are being given out.

- Miss a favourite lesson to make up work not done in another one.

- Send work home to complete.

- Complete a problem sheet.

- Write a letter of apology.

- Go and apologise in person.

- Wipe the tables in the dinner hall.

- Clean the desks in the classroom.

- Clean art equipment.

- Help with displays.

- Tidy books.

Isolation consequences

- Time-out table.

- One-minute detention at break, lunch or after school.

- Exit from class and work in another class.

- Sent to the Key Stage Leader or Head Teacher.

- Sent in from the playground for five minutes.

■ Sent to the touchline for one minute in a team game.

■ Exclusion or a managed move.

Other strategies that can be used in conjunction with these could include:

■ letter or telephone call home;

■ call the parents in for a meeting.

Select the consequences and decide how they will fit into your staged response within the classroom. This is a graduated system that begins with the least intrusive response and the least severe consequence. You will need planned steps that can be used depending on frequency and seriousness of the incident, ending up with either a referral on to the Key Stage Leader or isolation from the class.

Try to remain calm, dispassionate and level-headed when dealing with an incident. Begin by tactically ignoring and using redirection. Move on to rule reminders, then to warnings for any child who does not respond. A warning system should also have a stepped approach (see Figure 8.2).

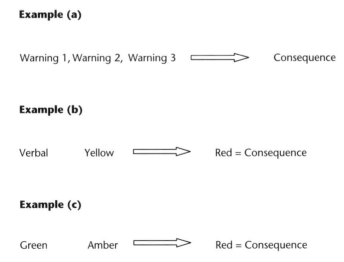

Example (a)

Warning 1, Warning 2, Warning 3 ⟹ Consequence

Example (b)

Verbal   Yellow ⟹ Red = Consequence

Example (c)

Green   Amber ⟹ Red = Consequence

Figure 8.2 Examples of stepped warning systems

Limit warnings to the lesson and start afresh when a new lesson begins. Children who get a verbal or a yellow warning (see Figure 8.2) but do not get as far as a red will have the slate wiped clean when the lesson ends. This allows pupils to start again and not give up early in the day if things go wrong. Children with deferred consequences will serve them later.

Recording consequences

Children do not like it when a teacher records an incident. Noting who did what and when is a powerful means of helping the whole class to behave well. None of them will want their name written in the book. Writing it down prevents forgetting who was involved in the heat of the moment.

There are a number of ways of keeping records. Teachers need a simple tool that serves the purpose, can be filed under the child's name and is easy to retrieve. For example:

Name	Verbal	Yellow	Red	Consequence	Reason
Andrews, S.	X				Out of seat
Brooks, P.					
Collins, B.	X	X			Talking
Dawkins, P.	X	X	X	One-minute detention	Talking
Finlay, S.	X				Out of seat
Frank, R.				Lose break	Swearing at Peter

Initially you will need sheets with all the names pre-printed because many of the pupils may get warnings during the establishment of your new behaviour code. Eventually you may find you need only a small record sheet for the day. For example:

Date 05.06.06

Lesson	Name	Verbal	Yellow	Red	Consequence	Reason
Literacy	Andres S.	x	x			Talking/ out of seat
Literacy	Collins R.	x	x	x	One-minute detention	Talking
Art.	Collins R.	x	x			Talking.

At the end of the day or week you transfer the details to each child's record sheet. This provides an ongoing record through the year (see – behaviour log in photocopiable materials).

There may be a time when a child in your class cannot turn their behaviour around, even after you have tried all of your strategies. Your only option left is to call for assistance and exit the child from the room. Sending a child out is the most serious sanction you can give and is the last resort. You would not think that when you see so many teachers sending children to their Head Teachers. It is a legitimate sanction and Heads should fully support a teacher who feels they need to use it but only if they have made every effort to help and include the child first.

▧ What do I do if a child has to be exited from the room?

All behaviour is a communication. Sometimes a child does not know how else to show their anxieties so they misbehave to get attention. It may be a cry for help but is often misinterpreted. We need to ask ourselves why the child is behaving in a particular way. The child will need time to cool off and then to talk to an adult or even another child to help them resolve their situation. This is best done away from the classroom.

Exiting a pupil may be your only option so you should plan how you will go about it. You should also explain to the children that it is one of the consequences and it is a very serious matter if it occurs.

You should not send a child to stand outside the room because it does not achieve anything except putting you in a difficult position. Who is supervising? The child may get distracted and wander off, resulting in an even bigger problem for someone else to deal with.

When there is no option but to exit a child, you should try to:

■ do it as unobtrusively as possible;

■ agree in advance with colleagues that it is all right to do so;

■ assign a place, perhaps with a senior colleague in another class, for the child to go to;

■ send work with the child. Do not expect the child to sit and do nothing. Do not expect a colleague to find the child work to do;

■ keep records of strategies you have tried, consequences given, details of what the child did and the reasons for exiting them.

Exiting a child can be stressful for you as well as for the other pupils, so it is a good idea to plan how you will go about it.

The procedure

■ Always warn the child of the next step and give a choice. Remind him of the rule, offer help, then allow some take-up time.

■ Stay calm, be assertive, but do not raise your voice. Showing you are in control and not getting stressed will have a beneficial effect on everyone involved.

■ Keep your distance. Do not go into the child's personal space. The length of your arm determines this. It is preferable to stand further back.

■ Avoid using threatening language. Give clear directions with choices and explain what the consequences will be if they are not followed. Suggest a good choice but do not give ultimatums. Make sure you stay within your school policy.

■ Children will read all of the signals you give off so try to appear relaxed. Use open-hand gesticulations and keep your hands at your side because a frightened child may think you have a weapon in your pocket. Try not to frown or appear angry. It is better to have a warm, friendly expression, which can be difficult in the circumstances.

■ Ask open questions to get the child talking and if possible, try to distract the child.

What should I do if the child will not leave the room?

Some schools have an advocate system; if so it could be helpful in a situation like this. Advocates are usually members of staff with a special responsibility for behaviour. They are generally not senior members of staff. Brief them when they arrive and then let them take over. They will talk to the child in a calm, quiet but assertive way. The change of face is often the key because the child has dug themselves into a hole that they cannot get out of. The new person helps them find a way out without losing face.

Many advocates have an agreed procedure for taking a child out of a class and then calming them down by helping them talk about the incident. They are experienced in showing the child how their behaviour changed during the incident and assisting them in re-examining the choices they had. They will talk about the choices and get the child to explore the consequences again to see whether they could find a better way to resolve things. The advocate will finish by helping the child to decide how to rebuild the relationship with the teacher and the rest of the children in the class. They may help him rehearse what he will say to them or draft out a letter of apology.

When there is no advocate or independent person available, an alternative strategy will be required. A child who digs in will act like a frightened animal. He may freeze or run. He may spit, snarl or stubbornly cling to fixed objects. He may even hide right inside or underneath things that you cannot access. A child who behaves in this way is probably seeking attention and feels that it is the only way to get it. In order to prevent them from succeeding and thereby reinforcing their behaviour it is necessary to isolate them. This is best done by exiting them. However, this sometimes proves to be impossible. Then, the strategy should be to take the rest of the pupils out and leave the child in the room.

The procedure

- Announce to the rest of the class that you will all be leaving the room to go to the hall, playground, library, computer room.

- Send a pupil for a colleague. Their role will be to stay with the child who is refusing to leave.

- Always have a fun activity up your sleeve for this eventuality. Things like team games, trust activities or parachute games are ideal and will quickly help the children forget the incident and get over the shock of what they have witnessed.

- Tell the class what you will be doing and make it sound fun.

- Remind the children of the directions for leaving the room and walking down the corridor.

- Leave the room once a colleague has arrived and the children are ready.

Use this checklist to ensure you have planned your procedure thoroughly:
- When will you use the exit procedure?
- Did you warn the child (not applicable for serious incidents)?
- What will you do if they refuse to leave?
- Have you organised the exit procedure with other staff and do you have advocates if you need them?
- Have you established a recording process?
- How will you follow up later?
- Have you involved the parents, Head Teacher and SENCO?
- What will be the consequence for the child?
- How will you rebuild the relationship with the child?

■ Review

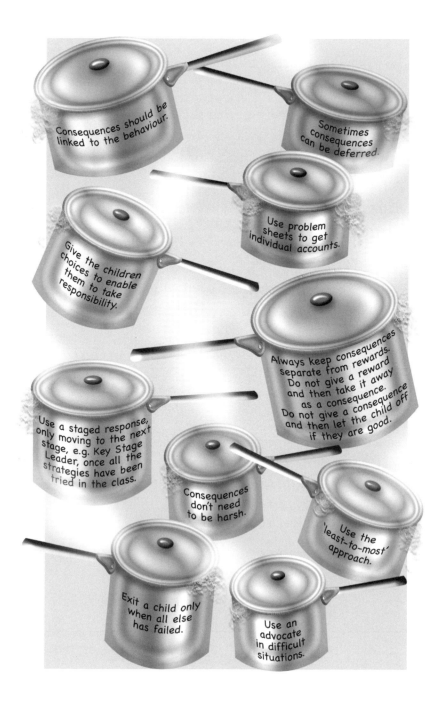

Consequences should be linked to the behaviour.

Sometimes consequences can be deferred.

Use problem sheets to get individual accounts.

Give the children choices to enable them to take responsibility.

Always keep consequences separate from rewards. Do not give a reward and then take it away as a consequence. Do not give a consequence and then let the child off if they are good.

Use a staged response, only moving to the next stage, e.g. Key Stage Leader, once all the strategies have been tried in the class.

Consequences don't need to be harsh.

Use the 'least-to-most' approach.

Exit a child only when all else has failed.

Use an advocate in difficult situations.

Chapter 9
Working with others

The education process is a complex one involving a team of people that can extend far beyond the school. As teachers, we are very aware of our role and the effect we have on the lives of our pupils. However, the responsibilities we take on often prevent us looking beyond the classroom and making the best use of the resources in the community. One of the most important aims a school should have is to try to give every child a memorable experience that they can cherish and carry with them through their lives. Such experiences are usually outside of the normal curriculum. They are the visits by organisations like the Army; trips out of school to unusual places like Parliament or newspaper printers; captivating activities such as pond dipping on a warm, sunny day or feeding goats at a local farm; and the uplifting moments like the school musical or the class assembly when all the parents applaud with expressions of pride. Teachers can turn a difficult thing like school into a magical experience for the children by utilising the help of others.

Teaching can be a lonely profession. Once the door is shut, you are in the company of thirty children for virtually the whole day. It is important to maintain and cultivate links with adults in the school and the wider community. You can establish a range of contacts that will enrich the work done in the lessons. The aim of this chapter is to identify them and offer suggestions for how they can be utilised.

School

It is easy to get totally absorbed in the work and not look beyond to see what is going on in the rest of the school. Traditionally primary school teachers have not had free periods that could be used to see what colleagues are doing in their lessons. This is now changing and opens up opportunities for learning and development through observation and discussion. It also provides scope for collaborative projects between colleagues and inter-class and cross-curricular activities can be more easily facilitated.

Starting work at a new school or as a newly qualified teacher can be a daunting prospect for some – exciting in many ways but still a challenge that may be stressful due to the uncertainties and the unfamiliar. If you have worked in a school for more than a year and are reading this, your role in helping new staff will be a significant one. Making them feel welcome on their first day and ensuring they know where the basic things are can make quite a difference. Most schools have an induction plan for new staff, but the quality can vary. The school may have a mentor programme, which can be invaluable in supporting staff in those early weeks. Newly qualified teachers (NQTs) usually have their own dedicated programme to enable them to complete their probation year successfully. Where there is more than one NQT, support groups with weekly meetings may be available. Whatever your position, make a point of linking up with others and meet informally as well as formally during breaks and after school to discuss common ground, share ideas and solve problems. Teachers usually want to help, it is in their nature. They welcome opportunities to get involved and work with colleagues outside of their room.

There are a number of useful networks outside of school that teachers can join. Your local education authority (LEA) will probably have termly meetings of subject coordinators to share good practice and resources. It is good to join these as they will put you in touch with other specialists in the subject.

A new initiative is the School Learning Network. This is designed to bring together groups of schools to work on particular developments that will raise standards. A cluster of schools will share resources and a budget to facilitate small working groups. Each group will be made up of staff from more than one school in order to disseminate the ideas and good practice that arise from the work they do together.

You should also try to contact staff in schools local to your own. Arrange to meet them and find out whether there are any opportunities to join together in activities. They may even let you work in a classroom either alongside a teacher or as a support assistant. This can be a rich experience, in that you will be able to pick up hints and tips and see alternative practices that will get you thinking about your own methods.

Local business

Partnerships with local businesses can yield a host of benefits. The value they can bring in enriching the curriculum is immeasurable. Many companies, especially the larger ones, have their own volunteer schemes. The staff are given time away from their normal responsibilities to work with other organisations. The regular commitment they can offer is well worth the time spent in advance in setting up the partnership.

Businesses can be involved with schools in many ways to enable children to be aware of and prepared for their own economic well-being such as:

- mentoring pupils;

- reading partner scheme;

- in-class support;

- mini-business enterprise;

- discussion groups about business and ethics as a part of the Healthy Schools Programme.

Trips out of school to visit particular business sites can be organised. Children enjoy things like:

- making a pizza at the local pizza restaurant;

- looking behind the scenes of banks and supermarkets;

- guided tours around factories, especially car manufacturers that use robot assembly lines;

- visits to newspaper printers or television studios.

Local businesses are usually very keen on associating themselves with schools, especially when they organise high-profile events that can offer mutual benefits. These can include:

■ maths challenges between schools;

■ gardening projects;

■ football coaching by the staff of a local professional team.

Companies can put up prizes, offer venues and lend equipment and even personnel to help you get going. Leisure centres are good providers of a wide range of additional sports activities along with your local outdoor pursuits centre (usually run by the LEA).

■ The community

The local area can be a rich source of resources that can enhance the school curriculum. Trips can be planned to museums, art galleries, churches, tourist attractions, farms and country parks. Organisations such as the National Trust, English Heritage and the Youth Hostel Association put on annual calendars of interesting and unusual events for children and schools.

Public-service organisations like the police, fire brigade, Army, ambulance service and road safety are all keen to work with schools on a diverse range of projects that promote a greater understanding of what to do.

Religious groups are usually happy to visit the school or invite parties of children to visit their places of worship. Establishing a good link with some of these enables children to become more familiar with their diverse interests and break down racial and cultural prejudice.

■ And last but not least, the parents and carers

These are our most important partners. It is vital that we work with them to promote positive relationships because they can make all the difference. Although the trend has been to make schools more open and get parents more involved, this may actually not be the case. Teachers have become busier, with greater workloads and more initiatives. Channels of communication may seem clearer but what could be happening is that it is becoming much harder to get a few words with a child's teacher. You need to seek out ways of establishing good channels of communication and building productive relationships. The following ideas may be useful.

Welcome/introduction letter

Taking over a new class has many problems and pitfalls. Avoiding the ones associated with parental anxiety is straightforward because it requires a short letter introducing yourself and outlining your expectations and plans for the term. This should be followed up with a brief induction meeting in September so the parents can visit their child's classroom and meet you and the support staff. Putting in the time and effort early like this will pay off later.

Home-school diaries

These can be invaluable in maintaining a useful and supportive dialogue between the teacher and the home. They can be time consuming because some parents will write long screeds day after day and expect replies. Split the task up with your support staff and decide how much time each day you can spend on routine messages. Always prioritise urgent messages such as issues of behaviour, a child's emotional state, requirements for school activities and things they may be forgetting to bring to school such as homework, reading books and PE kit. Make sure you ask parents to acknowledge things you have written. This can be as brief as initials and a date. Then you know they have read your note.

Class assemblies and school productions

These are the events that stay in the minds of many children and parents alike. They take a lot of time and effort and can be terribly frustrating, but they are well worth it on the day. Make an effort to ensure you involve all the children and rotate the major roles. Remember, a parent is probably looking only at their child, not the whole show, so give each child something important to do at least once in the year. Where more than one class is involved, do not make the mistake of having forty or fifty children in the chorus line or as extras. The best way is to agree a production idea with your colleagues and then have three class productions of it rather than three performances with the same cast. That allows a greater number to participate in the key parts.

Parents' evenings

These are the bane of some teachers' lives but they can be highly productive and rewarding. The report you give a parent is like a receipt for the taxes they have paid so they will want to feel satisfied. There are a number of important features of a good parent consultation session.

Be prepared

Prepare notes and have several pieces of work handy to illustrate what you want to say.

Keep to time

Plan what you want to say to fit the time. An appointment usually lasts ten minutes. This allows enough time for the following:

■ Introductions	1 minute
■ Current position (how the child is doing – National Curriculum levels)	1–2 minutes
■ Constructive praise	2–3 minutes
■ Targets the child is working on	2–3 minutes
■ Positive compliment about the child. Something personal that parents will appreciate	1 minute

Avoid opening the interview by asking the parent how they think things are going. They have come to find that out from you. Never over-run.

Current position

Give the parents the data for Numeracy and Literacy. They will want to know where their child is at the moment and how far they have moved up from the last assessment and whether the child is working at the expected level for their age. Keep this brief and avoid explanations at this point.

Constructive praise

Find something good to say about the child. There is always something, no matter how small. Children who make small steps may be putting in a huge effort. Parents will want to feel that you have noticed their child's achievements even if they know the child has not progressed as well as they should have done.

Targets

Share these with the parents. Show them you have worked out a systematic approach for their child and broken down their learning into small steps. This does not need to be negative. Learning involves mistakes and backward steps in order to move forward.

Always end on a positive note

Show the parents you care. Nearly if not all children in your class are capable of something and have their own gifts and attributes. Mention one of them and make it seem an important characteristic of their personality.

Make the meeting a supportive one. Do not use the session to be negative about the child. Of course, you must be honest, but do it in a sympathetic way within a positive framework outlined here.

To conclude, find ways to work collaboratively with the parents. Do not keep them at arm's length. Be open, honest and always remain professional. In that way you will win them over and together you will build a successful support group around the children to help them on their educational journey.

Review

Seek support from your colleagues.

Join subject groups in the LEA.

Make links with other teachers in the locality.

Use business links to enhance your curriculum.

Work with community groups to enrich your lessons.

Use local resources to bring subjects alive.

Build positive partnerships with parents.

Show you value every child by including them.

Final word

And finally, a few thought-provoking phrases:

- Every child is different. Every child matters.

- If a child has not learned it, it is not because they cannot – you just have not discovered the best way to teach it to them.

- Each pupil in your class is the pride and joy of their parents.

- School should be a positive experience and it is our job as teachers to make it a memorable one.

- Children get only one chance at their education.

BEHAVIOUR LOG

Class..........................   Date................................

Name	Verbal Warning	Yellow Card	Red Card	Consequence given

This questionnaire can be given to the child to complete either on their own, with a parent or with another member of staff. The scores may indicate a child has more than one preferred learning style. Each answer reveals a specific preference. For example, if the answer to question 1 is 'Yes' then that points towards an auditory learning style.

Name..   Class........................   Date..............

1.	I like listening to music	Yes	No
2.	I like drawing	Yes	No
3.	I like moving about	Yes	No
4.	I like watching films	Yes	No
5.	I like dancing	Yes	No
6.	I like acting	Yes	No
7.	I like making things	Yes	No
8.	I like chatting to people	Yes	No
9.	I like reading	Yes	No
10.	I like discussing things	Yes	No
11.	I like showing and telling the class about things	Yes	No
12.	I like going on trips	Yes	No
13.	I like making posters	Yes	No
14.	I like writing	Yes	No
15.	I like drawing diagrams	Yes	No
16.	I like talking while I work	Yes	No
17.	I like to go outside for lessons	Yes	No
18.	I like to watch videos in lessons	Yes	No
19.	I like listening to stories	Yes	No
20.	I like to speak to my friends	Yes	No

(After Garneth s.2002)

Date

Dear Mrs Brown,

I am writing to let you know how pleased I am with Sally's attitude and commitment to her studies in Art.

I run a scheme to reward students who exhibit the right behaviour and enthusiasm needed to do well. Sally has excelled in these requirements which has prompted me to inform you because I know how much pleasure it can bring to hear that one's child is doing well at school. I am extremely pleased with Sally's approach and if she continues in this way she will be developing valuable study skills.

Sally is showing a very conscientious attitude, doing her homework. She is working very well and I was particularly impressed by the way that she organised her time to get her homework in ahead of deadlines. I hope this letter brings you as much pleasure as it did for me sending it. You should be extremely proud of Sally and I look forward to reporting further successes to you.

Best wishes,

David Wright

Sally's teacher for Art

12th April 2007

Dear Mr & Mrs Brown,
I am writing to let
you know how hard
....
has been working
recently. He has made
a real effort to behave
well in my lessons.
You should be very
proud of him.

Yours sincerely
Mr David Wright
Class teacher

Affix
Stamp
Here

Here is a suggestion for a telephone call home to a parent:

> *'I really wanted to tell you how well Jane has been doing in my class. She has been putting a great deal of effort into her work and has produced some very interesting essays recently. She is setting a wonderful example to other students and her efforts have motivated them to try harder as well.*
>
> *'I am really pleased with her progress and know that she will go on to do extremely well if she keeps this up. You must be very proud of her. Could you tell her I rang?'*

References and bibliography

Bennathan, M. and Boxall, M. (1993) *The Boxall Profile. Handbook for Teachers*. London: Association of Workers for Children with Emotional and Behavioural Difficulties.

Caulby, D. and Harper, T. (1985) *Preventing Disruption: Practice and Evaluation in Urban Schools*. London: Croome Helm.

Cullingford, C. (1999) *The Causes of Exclusion: Home, School and the Development of Young Criminals*. London: Kogan Page.

Department of Health, Department of Education and Employment and the Home Office (2000) *Framework for the Assessment of Children in Need and their Families*. London: The Stationery Office.

Dreikurs, R., Grunwald, D. and Pepper, F. (1982) *Maintaining Sanity in the Classroom*. 2nd Edition. New York: Harper & Row.

Gardner, H. (1993) *Frames of Mind: The Theory of Multiple Intelligences*. London: Fontana.

Garnett, S. (2002) *Accelerated Learning in the Literacy Hour*. Leamington Spa: Hopscotch Educational Publishing.

Hughes, M. (1999) *Closing the Learning Gap*. Stafford: Network Educational Press.

National Primary Strategy (2005) *Excellence and Enjoyment*. 'Social and Emotional Aspects of Learning'. London: Department for Education and Skills (DFES).

Maslow, A. H. *et al* (1998) *Towards a Psychology of Being*. Chichester, West Sussex: Wiley.

Parsons, C. (1999) *Education, Exclusion and Citizenship.* London: Routledge.

Rendall, S. and Stuart, M. (2005) *Excluded from School.* London: Routledge.

Rogers, B. (1994) *The Language of Discipline. A Practical Approach to Effective Classroom Management.* Plymouth: Northcote House.

Smith, A. (1996) *Accelerated Learning in the Classroom.* Stafford: Network Educational Press.

Smith, P., Lovatt, M. and Wise, D. (2003) *Accelerated Learning: A User's Guide.* Stafford: Network Educational Press.

Smith, P. K. and Thompson, P. (1991) *Practical Approaches to Bullying.* London: David Fulton.

Wright, D. (1998) *Managing Behaviour in the Classroom. Practical Solutions for Everyday Problems.* Oxford: Heinemann.

Wright, D. (2005) *There's No Need to Shout. The Primary Teacher's Guide to Successful Behaviour Management.* Cheltenham: Nelson Thornes.

Index